The Book Cover Design:

The cover of the book was designed in collaboration between Anderson and Joan Wallace who volunteered to edit this book. Anderson has been communicating with Joan since she began reading the first draft of the book and he was instrumental in the design for the cover. Anderson explained the design to her as follows:

> *"The blue background represents the **Totality of Now,** the concentric light blue circles depict our **Oneness** and the kaleidoscope is there to remind you of your option to **Choose Again.** You merely need to shift your view ever so slightly to see all as it really is. And last but not least the reflection of the kaleidoscope is to remind you **To Reflect** prior to taking any action and ask yourself, "What is the most loving thing I can do in this moment?"*

> *"Be That One!"*
> *Anderson*

I0078781

Endorsements

"I don't know what to say except, BRAVO! To you and Anderson BRAVO! I know Anderson will speak again and again! I was blown away by the wisdom, depth and helpfulness of this book. You cannot just read this book, it will become one of those books that you will not want to loan out but keep to yourself, with all your underlining and notes, to read again and again. It's one of those books you can open to any section at random and soak in the wisdom and messages Anderson brings through you. You will want to buy a dozen copies for family and friends so they can share the wisdom in these pages. This was not brought through by the young man who laid down his body, but by the advanced soul that he was and is. There is no doubt this family had a soul contract or were involved in pre-birth planning to get this information out to help heal the consciousness of the planet. You, Lucy and Anderson are quite a trio. I am absolutely amazed at the helpfulness and insights contained in these pages. I loved Anderson Speaks and yet Anderson Speaks Again takes you to even higher levels of awareness. I would recommend this book to anyone seeking truth and a deeper awakening. The Course in Miracles influence is woven through it all, making it a lovely tapestry of truths. If Anderson Speaks Again doesn't become an international best-seller I will be surprised. It is the material best-sellers are made of. Bless you for being there for this soul to embrace and speak through."

Rev. Anne Puryear
Author of Stephen Lives!
and Messages from God

Anderson Speaks Again

Ushering in a New World

Anderson Skaggs
Narrated by Gene Skaggs

Anderson Speaks Again
Ushering in a New World
Anderson Skaggs
Narrated by Gene Skaggs, Jr.

Published By:
One Miracle
1140 Riverwood Drive
Nashville, TN 37216
www.onemiracle.org
www.geneskaggs.com

ISBN: 978-0-6156-8147-4

Cover designed by Anderson Skaggs and Joan Wallace

Printed in the United States of America
June 2012

This book is dedicated to my wife, Lucy, and our son, Jason

Table of Contents

Acknowledgements

It is with a great deal of love in my heart that I take the time to point out certain people who have helped to bring forth Anderson's second book. While writing the first book, <u>Anderson Speaks</u>, Anderson mentioned that there would be a series of books to follow. Although he could have given me all the information in one large book, he believes "The world has to be spoon-fed in the awakening process," thus the reason for this book and any sequels to follow.

The title of this book has changed. Originally it read "<u>Anderson Speaks Again: Life's a Journey, But We Need Not Walk Alone.</u>" During the editing process, the title changed to "<u>Anderson Speaks Again: Ushering in a New World.</u>" The original title seemed to fit with the first draft, but as the book unfolded, bringing forth messages concerning possible events centering around 2012, the titled changed.

I would like to thank my mother, Charo Hacker, for her help in the editing of this book. It gave her great pleasure to feel Anderson's presence. Also a big thank you to Janice Mickle for encouraging me to stay focused while bringing Anderson's messages to print.

With sincere love and appreciation, I want to thank my wife, Lucy, for constantly reminding me to bring forth these messages with Honor, Compassion, and Excitement. As she proofread the manuscript, she asked me to clarify certain messages. During this process Anderson revealed an additional section to expand the book. After writing the new section, I would report back to her with the additional information my sessions with Anderson brought forth. This allowed for a special communication between mother and son and continued their close relationship.

No matter how many times I have written this last "thank you," words still seem inadequate. As you can see on the inside cover, Joan Wallace is the person who came up with the cover for the book –

with guidance from Anderson. She has combined the most unique qualities of any individual that I have had the privilege to interact with. She is brilliant, spiritual, psychic and a founder of several non-profits too. It is a joy to watch her as she interlays these God-given attributes with Honor, Compassion and Excitement. Her love for her fellow brothers and sisters is mirrored in a way that emulates how God would like each of us to interact in this paradigm shift of "Living in Oneness."

Shortly after 2012 was welcomed in, I thought the book was complete and just needed to be proofed one more time. Once it was proofed, I was ready to write an acknowledgement section, come up with a cover, and it would be good to go. I proceeded to give the manuscript to three people whom I figured would complete the final proofing in a relatively short period of time. Joan noticed me handing out the manuscripts to those individuals and mentioned that she would like to read a copy. The reason I hadn't given her a copy of the manuscript was because she has an extremely demanding schedule, and I didn't want to impose.

A couple of days later she called me to mention that Anderson was speaking to her and gave her topics he felt I was blocking. These additional chapters were presented in a way that I could never have possibly conceived. The original manuscript was about 150 pages. As you can see, the additional chapters have increased the book considerably. Joan also rearranged the order of the chapters, and her editing was all done with the guidance and approval of Anderson.

I feel because of the urgency of revealing these messages the universe brought someone forward who could edit the book in the shortest possible time and get it out to the masses. After Joan mentioned that Anderson was speaking to her, I got still that night and asked Anderson about her editing the manuscript. He mentioned to me that the editing process was "out of your league." In addition, he informed me that I was to give her "carte blanche" in the editing process. After looking over the manuscript very carefully, I saw there was very little that was omitted.

Joan has demonstrated an unwavering commitment to present the book in a way that the world can embrace, and for this my heart is filled with joy! Because of the additional chapters that Anderson revealed to Joan, Anderson has expanded on an already fabulous book. Along with Joan's ability to communicate with Anderson, I feel that he accepted her as a child might acknowledge a parent.

Introduction

The Pain of Writing:

With a great deal of reluctance and a dash of procrastination, I have once again started a book with emotional pain. But I really would not have had it any other way. Why; because Anderson wants me to get his messages out to all who are willing to hear, and I will honor his request through every tear that will accompany the writing of this book. I knew the moment I picked up the pen in the writing of the first book that there would be a series of books that would accompany the first. But I put those thoughts on the backburner of my mind, trying to block out the inevitable, numerous tears I knew would accompany these writings. As always, when I finally said yes, a great deal of joy accompanied this decision. Writing and completing this book was no exception. Even with all my knowing, I still have times I cry out "Why?"

My process for writing this book begins with prayers and meditation. Thankfully, I am rarely awakened at two in the morning and given the information, as was Anderson's practice during the writing of the first book. In the morning, after I have done my meditations and prayers, I listen to a song or two of Anderson's and look at some of the pictures of him by the computer. I mean, I really look into his eyes and ask him, "What messages do you have for me today? What do you want the world to hear at this time?" Then I allow the energy to come into my body, usually accompanied with a tear or two, and say, "Okay, let's do it."

In the first book Anderson usually started our discussions by stating *"You people on planet Earth."* After one of our sessions I had thought that phrase was too impersonal and wondered why he had used it. In our next communication Anderson answered my question.

> *"I feel at some level most people misunderstand the verbiage of 'You people on planet Earth.' My awareness*

informs me that some of you feel it makes me separate from you, making you feel talked down to or somehow inferior. None of the above is true. I am your equal, but you still believe you live in time, and I am in complete awareness of the Totality of Now. When I use that salutation, I do so to acknowledge that our levels of perception and knowledge are different than most of those on planet Earth. So, of course, I will appear to have 'gifts' that my beloved counterparts on the other side of the veil have repressed."

I laugh at writing this last sentence as Anderson calls us his "beloved counterparts on the other side." It does seem to have a different ring to it than "You people on planet Earth." I enjoy the humor that Anderson infuses into the books. They are subtle reminders to smile and enjoy the process. As I reflected and smiled, Anderson then continued his dictation of the introduction to the book.

"Each chapter will be sufficient in and of itself. Because of the inclusiveness of the individual message, some information will be overlapped in various chapters, as well as within the same chapter. You will also notice that I will at times be telling Gene the same thing over and over. This is done for just the same reason; both he and you need to hear it more than once. This is done on purpose, as Truth needs to be heard over and over. Actually, the first time you hear anything you retain very little of the information, and it usually will not register in your mind until you experience what you have learned. So you will go through this book and think, 'Well, he has already said that before!' And I will say, 'Good for you for having noticed. Now really take another look at what has been said.' I have written it more than once because it is important, and I feel you needed to hear it more than once."

There is a tendency on my part to view some messages as having more significance than others. When that thought started to permeate my thinking, Anderson came to me and said,

"What seems to be common knowledge to one is rather monumental to another. In addition, people have preferences as to how they can accept a certain message. It makes little difference as to which venue they choose. Some will only accept the information from someone who has a list of credentials behind their name. With others the information will have to come from a certain religion or from other various formats. Finally, there are those who will embrace the Totality of Now in their awakening process through reading these books. Honor all paths, all choices. Why; because they are all your brothers and sisters and your equals in every way. Please lay down the judgment that one path is of greater value than another."

Obstacles in Writing the Book:

Most people that write usually have a dominant topic they are addressing and have an idea of what they want to present the reader. Every day when I start writing I have no idea where it is going to take me. The only thing I am aware of is that I will write what Anderson wants me to write, regardless of how I feel others may perceive these messages. In the taking down of these messages there are times when the messages are directed exclusively for me, my family members or someone specifically that Anderson wants to reach. I have chosen to omit the ones that are too personal or might invade the privacy of the individual. Otherwise, the book includes all the topics that Anderson wanted covered.

On a personal note, it has been over two years since Anderson passed, and I have had time to reflect on our new relationship, my interactions with him, and how it has affected every area of my life. The best way for me to describe the continuous grieving process, and it is ongoing, is the feeling of losing a body part. You learn to cope, manage the feelings and carry on, but the evidence of the loss is always with you. I do the best I can. It is easier at times, but the grief can come back at any moment. I truly try to give all my interactions a divine purpose, but at times the missing of his physical presence still comes to the forefront and derails what I am doing. It is then that I remind myself once again of why he came. I know that is what I am supposed to do, and I will honor my part in our relationship with all my heart.

> *"Dad, you and I are speaking of the physical body you call 'Gene' who needs to become as pure a channel and vortex for messages to come forth. The clearer the channel, the purer the messages will come forth. You are very clear in most areas, but you still want to judge what messages the world is ready or not ready to hear. You have to put that judgment aside. You are usurping your authority when you do that.*
>
> *This 'control' comes from a previous life where you had great spiritual gifts and had not always used them wisely. You really didn't abuse them, but you didn't use them to the fullest advantage for the planet. That guilt still weighs on you, and you feel that you can atone for it by controlling which messages come forth and which ones YOU choose to deem unworthy for the planet to hear at this particular time.*
>
> *I want to say that in the messages you have allowed, you have been a clear channel, but it is time to stop judging which ones need to come forth. I know you can see this clearly, especially since you have allowed yourself to be 'exposed' to your readers so that they can view some of your repressed issues. This 'exposing' has caused certain repressed issues to come forth and be cleared. We are happy that you have agreed to this internal clearing."*

After re-reading the above information Anderson had given me, I asked him, "How can I allow these topics to come forth that you are so desperately trying to give me?" I didn't receive an answer right away to the question so I went back to writing. As soon as I did, Anderson came back to tell me,

> *"Go ask Lucy which chapters you are blocking."*

Therefore, some of the chapters you see in the book came from Lucy's personal conversations with Anderson. Although these conversations were accompanied with a great deal of pain, she had the willingness to "fight" through her pain to come up with these topics. I would like to thank her for her willingness to bring these subjects to the forefront and put them here in this book.

Messages of Encouragement to Write:

Today, as I listened to some music and looked at Anderson's pictures to help me get in touch with him, an overwhelming sadness covered me as a blanket covers one from the cold. I felt that I either couldn't or didn't want to go on and that I had little reason to do so. Intuitively I knew my purpose and mission, but at the time that information was in my head and not in my heart. So I asked Anderson for his help to get me through these feelings.

> *"Don't look at your feelings of despair as a failure, rather the natural process on your planet as you go through all the issues attached to the grieving process. Always invite me to be with you while you have these feelings. Picture me with you, feel me, and, as I stated in the previous book, this will be no idle fantasy.*

> *Be kind to yourself. Notice how these unworthy feelings are becoming less and less prevalent and not as severe when they do occur. Remember why you are here, honor the tears, and remember I am as close as your breath and only a thought away.*

My Hope for the Readers:

It is my wish that this book and the others Anderson will bring forth enable you to see yourself as no longer a slave to time or to physical limitations but as a spiritual being in control of your life. You are the captain of your ship. If you follow the guidance within this book, it will allow the wings of love to open your heart to the unlimited joy available to you. I hope Anderson's messages will give you hope for both your personal life and, as importantly, for Mother Earth. As in the first book I have listed Anderson as the author, and, once again, that is the honorable thing to do.

Chapter 1: Anderson

Our Anderson:

My beloved son, Anderson, at the age of 22 laid his body down. It's been over two years since, and in looking back over Anderson's life I have come to realize how I took so many things for granted. He was the most perfect being that I can describe. I am not saying that just because he was my son. I am very capable of looking at unhealthy traits in myself and family members. He always had something good to say about others, was an honor student, a college graduate, and an excellent athlete. He was a loving, loyal, and compassionate person. He worked each summer with kids and adults that were mentally and physically challenged. It never ceases to amaze me that even after his death he is still trying to bring forth messages to help his fellow brothers and sisters on planet Earth.

Anderson Speaks From Beyond:

In the first book Anderson mentioned his ultimate reason, as well as numerous others, for the laying down of his body. Anderson was born to be a healer, and he knew that before he chose to incarnate on this planet. His death is part of an overall plan in the unfoldment that is presently taking place on this planet.

Anderson laid his body down on a Thursday evening, and two days later he came to me with his Original Seven Messages. (Please refer to that particular chapter in his first book Anderson Speaks.) The way the first and subsequent messages were relayed to me was that his energy would come from behind me and merge with mine. The energy would encompass my very being, and we would merge into a single entity. I would usually sit at my computer, look at some of his pictures and say something in the order of, "Okay, what messages do you have for me at this particular moment?"

There were other ways I would receive his messages, such as dreams and his audible voice. Whenever I received his messages audibly, they were usually urgent and not necessarily messages that he wanted to go in the book. Most of these messages were directed to something that had happened to me personally. These discussions were usually specific to interactions between Anderson and me. Because I feel that others can identify with these messages I've included some of them in this book. These messages will show the reader that those on the other side of the veil are constantly trying to teach us a better way to interact with one another. They are meant to help remove the self-imposed obstacles we place between ourselves and our Creator.

Some of the topics included in this book were initiated by Anderson, and others were in answer to my questions or topics that I wanted included in the book. The writing of this book has been a process in which I have rarely been able to sit down and write without some sort of internal growth taking place. Tears and joy are all part of taking down these messages. And, again, my emotions seem to run the gamut, but they are always accompanied with a distinct sense of purpose.

Choosing to Experience the Loss of a Child:

Some would ask, "Why would you choose in this incarnation to experience the loss of a child?" As I mentioned earlier, Anderson stated that I have been a good vortex for the messages, but there were still some chapters that I was blocking. I felt the chapter on *HONOR, COMPASSION and EXCITEMENT* was one of them.

One Thursday night before class began; a lady came early to the group and brought up the same question of experiencing the loss of a child to me. I smiled inside, as I have heard this question numerous times from Lucy but only a few other times from others. I told her, "Just a moment. I'd like you to, please, ask the question of Lucy." When Lucy had finished getting ready and walked in the room, I told Lucy this student had a question for her. She asked Lucy the question again, and Lucy looked at me and said, "I know I've asked Gene that question a thousand times." That's when it hit me. I needed to ask Anderson that question.

"Remember nothing happens by accident. Everything is a result of your thoughts. If that is true, and it is, then you are the maker of your world. Remember the chapter on Cause and Effect. Your most basic law states that you can't have an effect without a cause.

So if you're thinking you are the cause of all events on your viewing screen or world, and there is no exception to this, then what you see in your world you will know that you have put there. Ultimately, the reason these things are there is rather irrelevant. Hopefully, you are starting to see how your thoughts go forth and permeate all areas of your life, but there is even more to know about cause and effect.

At a level that very few are capable of remembering, before you made the choice to incarnate, you decided what gender you would be and the parents who would birth you. You also knew a basic outline of what events you would come up against in this particular incarnation. Nothing is completely carved in stone, as you have free will at all times. Sometimes because of certain circumstances you chose to alter why you have come. Some of the more dominant events that occur to you can change in how they are played out in this particular incarnation. Generally, any process of changing our life's purpose after you have incarnated usually comes from a place of fear from within you.

But there are those that come to this planet, look around and decide to take on a more humanitarian role than their original purpose. Once again, that is rather rare, as most people on Earth pretty much follow the script that has been outlined for them on the other side of the veil. Whenever one chooses a role that has global ramifications, then this new role usually requires them to

3

overcome major obstacles. The main reason for this is that anyone that goes against their society norms will be viewed as radical, and as such would naturally come up against obstacles that others would have avoided.

We are not going to go through all the possible reasons why someone would choose to experience certain events in their life. That really would be a whole other book and would take you away from the messages we are trying to set forth here. But, ultimately, why one chooses to allow a certain event to play out and in this case the choice to have a child leave the planet before you is what we will focus on in this chapter.

Everyone wants to know why their child died. Actually, knowing why solves very little, if anything. What knowing does for you is it gives you a reason to allow their choice to leave this planet a chance to manifest itself in a divine manner. We want to express very strongly that knowing why solves nothing and always emanates from the egoic part of your mind. For example, you know why your car won't start. It has a dead battery. That really doesn't fix the car, but you do know the reason why. There really is no singular answer to this question or others, as your heart cries out with such questions as, 'Why would someone choose an incarnation in which their child leaves this Earth plane while they still have a body?'

The first thing We would like to mention here is your child's decision to lay their body down was done with your mutual consent. They chose it for countless reasons, but I want you to remember that all you really have conscious control over is your emotions surrounding this choice your child has made. I am aware that most people have similar thoughts of, 'What could I have done differently?' 'Why has God punished me?' Of course, there are others, but the most dominant question is simply 'Why?'

Even if you know why, that doesn't ease the pain. You know why I had to leave. It is stated very clearly in the first book, but you still cry "Why?" There is only one reason for the asking of why – this is applicable for anyone facing a similar event in their life – and that is their inability to give what has happened a divine purpose. Until one does just that, the healing process will lay dormant. They will continue to ask why, and even if they know why, the pain is always in the forefront.

So We ask with a great deal of love and compassion for anyone facing a similar situation in their lives to give that event a divine purpose. Just ask, 'Show me what the underlying purpose is.' Then tell yourself, 'I will give the laying down of the body a divine purpose. I don't know what that is or what it will look like, but I am willing to be shown.' To the degree that you mean what you say, then the divine purpose will be revealed to you. The divine purpose usually doesn't mean something on a grand scale. Most of the time, they will be day-to-day happenings. Say to yourself, 'I will give this event a divine purpose. Please show me how I can express HONOR, COMPASSION and EXCITEMENT around this event.'

We are not saying tears won't fall, they will. But the singular event of giving it a divine purpose will gradually unveil what your new role has become pertaining to the laying down of the body. The joy of watching your new purpose unfold will be the joy you have previously thought impossible.

This part is strictly for you, Madre. You have done this before in another lifetime, and each time there was pain involved in the decision. Not on the other side, because each time you have rejoiced in knowing you would play a pivotal role in a major shift on the planet. But when you incarnate, you forget what you have done, and that is very normal because you get caught up in not wanting it to unfold because of the love attached to the one you have

5

brought forth. This will be your last time in a similar role,
but you have a major role now that I have laid down my
body. As we mentioned in previous chapters on the
feminine role, this aspect of Love will escalate on your
planet, and there will be people that can only hear these
messages attached to a female voice. Be that One! Love,
Anderson!"

Anderson as My Teacher:

The topics discussed in this chapter are taken from experiences that I learned while talking to Anderson about issues in my personal life. The messages were directed to me, but as you will see, the messages are also universal. I would like to thank Anderson for helping me through my "mundane" topics as well as those that have brought up feelings of loss no one should have to experience.

Lucy and I took a much deserved vacation in mid-July of 2011, and we didn't take the time to either write or make contact with Anderson until about three weeks afterwards. Lucy and I came together to do a meditation for the singular purpose of connecting with Anderson. It was a Sunday morning, and after the meditation I decided to take a look and see how the garden was coming along. I was amazed by how well everything was doing, as we were already giving away excess cucumbers. We also had about 14 or 15 tomato plants, and up until that time we were just getting enough tomatoes for ourselves but not enough to share with friends. As I looked around, I noticed there were about 8 to 10 tomatoes that were getting red all at once, and there were literally hundreds that were going to be ready in the following weeks. As I thought about giving all those tomatoes away an overwhelming joy came over me. It was at this point that Anderson visited me and said:

"The garden is a nice metaphor about your life. In fact,
the garden represents your life. You have to till the garden
and get it ready, which means you have to interact with
your brothers and sisters in such a way that will produce

love and joy in your life. Then you have to plant the seeds
or the small plants, which translates into you becoming
aware of your thoughts, as each thought brings forth fruit
which mirrors that particular thought. You have to weed
the garden, which translates into you having to remove
those thoughts that bring forth undesirable interactions in
your life. And once you are done, you have to step back
and allow the garden to grow, which translates into you
allowing your Creator to be in charge of your life.

Do not assume you know what is right for either yourself
or your brothers and sisters. That is extremely difficult for
you to grasp, as most people want to have control over
what takes place in their life. Just stop and think for a
moment, do you think you can do a better job than God?
We smile as We see the little ego's hand going up.

If you do something without guidance from your Creator,
you have usurped your authority and assumed a position
that has no merit. This will always bring pain to the
surface sooner or later, a lesson which you have taken to
heart. Be proud of that and show others in a gentle
fashion this most important lesson.

Look at all those tomatoes; they represent all the gifts that
God has presently given you. Take notice of how you
thought about giving them away, and the joy it brought
you. That is God expressing Herself through you.
Anything that comes from God always comes in excess
and has to be given away. Notice that if you don't give the
tomatoes away, they will spoil. Well, the same thing holds
true for the gifts of God."

At that point I thought about how correct his last statement was
and knew that is how life is supposed to be. God always gives in
excess, and the joy emanates and extends itself when we give that
excess away. And then Anderson reappeared again and told me:

"That is the definition of joy: One has so much that one has to give it away or it will spoil."

I thought this was the end of this topic, but his final thought came shortly afterwards.

"If you are not giving away the excess good that God has given you, what you have will spoil, but just as importantly, you will block the future flow of that particular gift."

Chapter 2: The Purpose of this Book

Anderson's Messages and Style:

Some of the topics that were in the first book can also be found within this book. Anderson explains this as:

"The world will have to be spoon-fed during the awakening process. Each subject that crosses over into this book will have added insight. The reason for this, My Beloved Brothers and Sisters, is that you really only have one problem, but because you think you have many, we have to answer you in various ways. When you start to see the commonality in all problems, your awakening will have begun and your understanding will continue to expand. Once you begin down this path, your view of everything will change drastically. You will gain clarity in your life's purpose, and understand what was always intended for each of your interactions with others. At that point your ego's need 'to be right' will vanish."

When Anderson uses of the word "I" within his messages, this means the messages are strictly coming from Anderson. When he uses the word "We/Our" he will be referring to a group or cluster of deities or spiritual leaders on the other side, all with the same purpose:

"Our purpose is the healing of planet Earth accompanied by the complete remembrance of the Totality of Now. 'The Totality of Now' is used to describe GOD within our True Reality of the multidimensional Now while Being In Oneness. This multidimensional NOW includes all aspects of time: past, present and future, which are all occurring right now. Our true 'Oneness' includes all living things, which are also a part of an extension of God.

*Our 'Oneness' is the remembrance that we are part of
God and God is part of us, and, as such, we have access
to all his knowledge. (If you were to take the concept of
Oneness as shown in the movie Avatar and expand upon it
to include all living things within the universe, you would
be on the right track to understanding 'Oneness.') One of
the most important concepts to grasp within this book is
that all living things are a part of God."*

Anderson's Purpose for the Book:

It is with a great deal of joy that I write this book on behalf of
Anderson. Please take what I am about to say with Love. There are
times when I am conflicted about what I am about to say. At times I
feel we need a God in flesh form, someone we knew and who walked
among us, someone who has breathed the air we are breathing,
someone who has faced all the obstacles thrown at us, so that when we
pray or ask for help, we have a picture to associate where this divine
intervention is coming from. So if it helps you to picture Anderson
guiding you as you read this book, I am sure that will be no idle fantasy
as he constantly reminds me, "I am as close as your breath."

*"First, I would like to thank Gene, my beloved father, for
having the courage to take down these messages the world
so desperately needs to hear. He mentioned in the
previous book that he doesn't enjoy writing nor considers
himself a writer. It makes little difference as to where
these fears come from. What is of importance is that he is
able to lay them aside and do what We have assigned him
to complete.*

*He truly has accepted his part in the unfolding of a new
reign on your planet. Much will be 'thrown' at him, and
with Our help he will bring them into manifestation. He
now knows that is because we made a deal/pack before
either of us chose to be in a bodily form to bring these
divine messages to the world. He also knew that I would*

lay my body down at an early age and the pain that would entail.

I also know that Lucy, my beloved Madre, knew what this incarnation would entail, and I want to thank her for having the courage, once again, to put herself in this position.

I have a divine appointment to bring a paradigm shift to this planet that will change the way we interact with ourselves, each other, and Mother Earth. To expedite this process, the form I have chosen to take on this planet has brought a great deal of pain to my parents, my brother, other family members, and friends. I am deeply sorry for your pain, but, please, rejoice with me in what I am doing.

Actually, my joy and my union with others on the other side of the veil is imperative at this time. These messages have to be brought forth, and thus the need for these paradigm shifts. The world truly does not have the luxury of the old antiquated ways of trying to align with who they are as created by God. You do not have the time, and time, as you have experienced it, is collapsing at a rate the world has never seen.

As I mentioned in the previous book, keeping me on this planet would be like keeping your child in kindergarten. You know where your child is, you know they are safe, but that is not who they really are. To love someone you must be able to set them free to be what one's Creator has intended them to be. Please be happy for me. My only purpose is for you to experience the Totality of Now, the true essence of your being. When one knows that, the form in which it gets expressed becomes irrelevant.

I jumped for this assignment, and my father jumped with me. I know he still cries. I know he still wishes things on this planet could have been different. Listen to what I have heard him tell others, 'If I could wave a magical wand

11

and have Anderson back, I would not do it. I know why he came, I know why he left, and I know what I am supposed to do. I know what Lucy is supposed to do, and I will honor that with all my heart.' But from an Earthly fatherly perspective he would answer, 'I would want him back. But I love him with a love that has no parallel on this planet.' This is what should pass for love on your planet, and this is how it should look. I ask each of you to re-read what he just wrote.

As in the first book, there is no political stance taken, nor are there views as to one religion being better than another. Nor will this book or sequential books speak specifically on the Earthly changes, other than to say times will be changing at a very fast rate, and Earthly shifts are subject to change, and the severity of the change is also subject to change. Although it is of imperative importance, this book will not be the format. There are others who will bring those messages to your planet.

Actually, in 2012 little will take place, as we are in the dawn in the awakening process. Yes, shifts will occur, but as you will read, most will be inner shifts, and, of course, subject to change from individual to individual based on how they have honored their divine purpose at this time. The actual timeframe of major shifts is more in the order of late 2014 to 2015.

Hopefully, this book will not be compared to other similar books. Comparison is always of your ego, and one will have to make a judgment as to one thing being better than the other. Each book, each doctrine, each religion, each modality needs to stand on its own merit.

My father has no supernatural powers. His gifts are available to all of you, and all that you lack is the awareness of them. His purpose does not allow him to channel others on the other side, unless it will be beneficial for both parties. At the present time this would

12

take away from his 'assignment.' At a later date things could change. So upon reading this book or the first book, unless you are extremely guided to do so, please do not seek him out to get in touch with a loved one that has passed away. There are many others out there that have been endowed with that talent.

The mere fact that you are reading this book is no accident. If you feel you need someone to help you make contact with someone on the other side, simply ask me and I will arrange for the right person to come into your life. If one reads the first book, there are a couple of places where I give you techniques on how to make contact with those on the other side.

At times some of the messages in this book will be straightforward, and at other times they will have playfulness about them. Do not let the playful nature of a message detract from its importance. Each message has great significance.

Because you feel you live in a world that contains individual bodies with separate needs and desires, you live by comparisons. Therefore, We will have to speak to where you think you are. So comparisons will overlay a great deal of our conversations with my beloved brothers and sisters because that is what you can understand. Once you put aside these senseless beliefs, then and only then can you finally come to realize there is nothing to compare yourself. Because of your inclusive Oneness with everyone and everything, you will realize you have been what you are searching for all along. Therefore, it truly is a journey without a distance, because you will eventually come back to the starting point.

There will be a very strict code that my father will be following, and his singular purpose from this time forward cannot waiver. Because of this, We have brought a little drama up in his life for the sole purpose of clearing certain unresolved issues that were still present from past incarnations. As of this writing, it is all removed. I would like to thank those people for allowing this process to take place. It is rather rare on your planet that We will bring something up on your side of the veil to be cleared. This is only done when something of such magnitude needs to be presented to your planet.

The normal process of drama that takes place on your planet is normally caused by both parties' inability to address their repressed fears. This will be covered in this book as well as various books that will be forthcoming.

Some of the material in this book has been given to your planet in some format at one time or another, but there is also information in here that has never touched the ears of this generation. Each generation is fed the information in ways they can understand. Information that is fed for a certain sector of people will have to be presented in a certain format, or they will be unable to hear and accept the information.

Because of the illusion of time, it will appear that the messages are expanding with each birthing. That is only because one can only hear what one is ready to hear. Science is allowing a greater expansion of Truth. People will believe certain message if science can validate what is being said. Many spiritual concepts have been proven, and many have yet to be proven by the scientific community and some, science will never be able to validate. Science can only prove what they believe. Their results, therefore, are hampered by their beliefs. So the scientific community will have to have people who believe in certain spiritual laws to prove that these spiritual laws do exist.

Once again, seldom do We intervene on this side of the veil, but because of the imminent events that will be taking place on your planet, We will circumvent events and time

14

by 'placing' certain people within the scientific
community to expedite messages that otherwise might
have taken generations to finally be looked at seriously."

As of this writing I have heard from numerous people that I know and some whom I have never met letting me know that Anderson has contacted them and given them messages. At first I was rather amazed, but once I had time to reflect, my heart would light up with joy. Anderson is still Changing Lives.

Except for a couple of small sections, the remainder of the book is all written coming from Anderson. While the book has undergone some editing, the messages have stayed pure. I hope that you will enjoy reading the book as much as I have enjoyed taking it down for you.

The Unreality of Death:

"The word 'death' for most seems to have a finality
associated with it. But in observing your planet, death
actually signifies a birth of some things. Leaves fall and
die but prepare the ground for future trees. Whatever dies
has to form a vacuum for something else to take its place.
You live in a world of opposites, so the opposite of death
is life. But, in reality, birth and death just play out a
picture of love on a glorious screen you call Earth.
THERE IS NO DEATH. There is only a re-birthing of
something from the invisible to the visible world, just a
changing of a vibration that allows your eyes to see or to
stop seeing!

You feel something dies when your eyes can no longer see
it. What is really taking place is the thing that appears to
have gone simply has rearranged its frequency and is now
on what most would call the invisible side. It doesn't mean
it no longer exists. It just means the frequency at which
most are accustomed, are not in the range where one can
presently see what has been displaced. When you are in

15

alignment with the Totality of Now you will have the capacity to see everything that ever permeated your planet. The veil that separates the two worlds will disappear. When you stop associating yourself as a body, you open yourself up to communicate with anyone that ever walked this planet.

The topic of death, the unreality of death, will more likely be read by people coming from some type of Christian background. Actually, whether you have a Christian background or another background just about everyone on this planet has heard of Jesus. He is the one person who crosses all religions, even the nonbeliever has heard of Jesus. When Jesus laid his body down, did who he was, the central core of him, die? Of course not, everyone will have to see the obvious answer to the preceding rhetorical question. Who he was, and is, has not changed.

Jesus is available to anyone who inquires. The same is applicable to anyone else that has ever walked your planet. When you lay aside your identification with your body, a whole new world opens up and those on the other side of the veil become available to you. Why; because you now realize the illusionary nature of the veil. In reality, there is no veil. This veil that we talk about, that religious leaders have written and spoken about, truly doesn't exist. It is a story made up by the ego in an attempt to explain our spirit side to the body's mind.

The veil is a screen, a kind of vaporous screen that those who have identified themselves within a limited self-imposed body have manufactured to keep themselves from love. Because of its illusionary nature, contact with those on the other side of the veil, those you called dead, can occur without the laying down of the body.

As We stated in the Foreword, you live your life in contrast. Actually, how could you not? The body is the manifestation of contrast. If there is life, there has to be

16

*death; if love, there has to be hate; if cold, there has to be
a contrasting temperature by which to judge. Therefore,
when you identify with something, you then have to push
yourself away from the opposite of your identification. If
one has laid their body down, you feel subconsciously that
you can no longer have communication with that person.
That is simply a choice in belief, and, as such, you can
simply choose otherwise.*

*We would like to state that the word 'choose' is probably
the most empowering word We can use. Everything is a
choice, and you always have the choice to choose love, or
the alternative, which is fear. The alternative choice of
fear is based upon the concept of the false self you have
made up within your ego. Love and fear are on the
opposite ends of the frequency spectrum.*

*To understand frequencies, one might want to look at your
radio, and how there are different stations. Each station
sends out its signals at a certain frequency. There are two
types of frequencies, AM and FM. Within each frequency
there are various stations, but all are emitting from either
the frequency of AM or FM. These frequencies are all
around you, but you can't hear them unless you turn your
radio on and set it to the particular channel you want to
listen.*

*Just because you don't have your dial adjusted to your
station doesn't mean it is turned off or not transmitting.
This simply means you can't hear it because YOU are not
in alignment with that particular frequency. It really isn't
that hard. You simply have to understand that the
frequency or vibration of the other side of the veil is Love,
and you have to want love more than you want fear.
Sometimes when faced with the loss of a loved one, one
can actually be in a good place to choose love over fear
because the pain is so unbearable. Ask your lost loved one
for their help. Who they are, their true essence is still*

available to you, and they would be ecstatic for you to reach out to them.

In your world you have been taught that death is the opposite of life. With that in mind, opposites cannot come together; they actually are repelled by one another. Also the word 'death' is associated with the word 'finality.' That is why the word 'energy' is so crucial in trying to explain everything We so desperately want to get across. You are pure energy, but your energy resonates at such a low frequency once it manifests itself into a body that most cannot communicate with the other side. Your scientists are proving some of what We are speaking of today and will eventually be able to prove most of the things presented in this book.

Death is associated with a body and the laying down of a mass of matter. You are not your body, you are energy, and We should put that word with a capital 'E'. Because, ultimately, what you are is Divine Energy and this Energy can never dissipate. It is unlimited; you can never use it up. It is constantly expanding, constantly giving, and constantly guiding you. You are the captain of your body. You can navigate it through rough waters or calm seas. But you are the captain, not the ship. When the body's usefulness is achieved on this planet, one can simply lay it down, and with great joy move on to other endeavors.

This Energy, the true essence of who you really are, has not actually changed in any manner when the body is laid down. On this side of the illusionary veil that permeates your planet you will come to realize this Energy is like a wave that flows across your mind, as the wind blows the leaves of a tree during a warm summer breeze. This Energy is constantly moving and expanding. It is always giving and never vacillates from its true nature of Love.

The reason this description of your true self feels so strange to most is that you have identified love as being *separate from that which you truly are. Many believe love is something they have to acquire or earn and definitely is not automatically your unconditional true inheritance. After all, how could you possibly be Divine Energy? I say unto you, 'How could you not be this Divine Energy?'*

You believe you can chop up Love in little pieces, identify with that piece, claim it as your own, and, therefore, identify other pieces as being love that you have or don't have and is, therefore, separate from the Totality of Now. How insane to think one can take dualism into a non-dualistic thought system, which is what Love is, and make it real. Only the arrogance of your ego could possibly contrive of such foolishness. Who you are, the true Essence of your being is one with everything, and We mean everything. Your essence is not just what your body's eyes can see, but everything that ever was, is or will be in the future.

Once again, I realize this and many of the other topics are hard to picture or imagine, but that is because you are trying to picture infinity with a finite mind. You have to be shown something beyond what your present mind can grasp. It needs to be stretched. You cannot get ready for these shifts that are going to take place with your present mindset. The understanding of these topics will occur when you are willing to see only the good in yourself, everyone else, and in everything.

We truly understand you can't comprehend some of these topics, and, actually, We are not asking you to understand them. Because given where you are on this imaginary ladder back to Oneness, your mind can't wrap itself around some of these spiritual laws. But all We ask is a little willingness to see your brothers and sisters as yourself, see what's in their hearts, and see what they are crying out for. If you are willing to do this – actually that is all you are capable of – then your repressed thoughts that speak to you will vanish as does the dew in the

19

*morning sun. It is in the extending of love under all
situations that the meaning of Love is revealed. Each
spiritual law We are setting forth is merely an aspect of
Love. Be that One!"*

Our True Essence:

*"Our True essence has nothing to do with who We are as
defined by our persona. Ask someone to describe who
they are, and they will usually start out by saying what
they do for a living, where they live, their race, gender,
material status, religion, etc. All of this has nothing to do
with who you are. You are a child of God, here to birth
and bring forth God in flesh. I know that sounds like a
rather bold statement, but until you accept your role, you
will continue to identify with your persona and always
feel the pain and disappointment associated with that
attachment.*

*Once you have accepted your true Essence is connected
to your feelings, then a deep, indescribable feeling of love
will come forth. This love can then be shared with all your
brothers and sisters, not just those 'special' loved ones.
This really isn't difficult. In fact, it is the easiest thing to
do because it is the only natural thing you can do.*

*Some of you have done a magnificent job of developing a
defense against this love, i.e. your egoic thought system.
You employ this egoic thought system to keep you from
remembering who you really are. So be cautious when
you say you cannot learn what you are here to do because
you have taught yourself a most complicated thought
system that will try to prove otherwise.*

*The Holy Spirit's thought system is easy because its only
purpose is to help you to remember who you are. And*

with this knowledge that you are here to help others, you must also remember who they are. You will have all the help you need. All you have to say is, 'Okay, I am willing to head in the direction of Love.' When you say that and MEAN that, We will arrange everything on this side of the veil to bring that into manifestation. Be that One!"

Channeling Messages:

"The words 'Psychic abilities' cover so many topics that one would need a book to truly cover all the different aspects around the subject matter. The aspects of the psychic that I will cover for you will be the ones that will be of most benefit in getting the messages out that We want the planet to hear. We have a singular purpose for you in this incarnation and will never deviate from the course of action needed to bring it forth. I will use this definition for the word 'psychic': Any thought derived from non-sensory gauges. Of course, when referring to 'sensory' I am referring to your five senses.

Once again, there are others out there that will be in alignment with other psychic traits, and one is not of any more worth than another. All psychic powers should be used for the singular purpose of extending love and helping oneself and others remember who they are. If you don't use these gifts as intended or you use them for self-gratification, then neither the giver nor receiver will benefit from the exchange. Once again, I will focus on what will be beneficial for you with your particular assignment in this incarnation.

These talents have lain dormant within you, as with most others on your planet, but it will take little to dust them off and bring them to your conscious awareness. I smile as I see you stepping out of the self-imposed box that has surrounded you most of your life. You, as most on your

21

*planet, feel your persona is yourself. You feel the box is
safe in the seeming illusionary protection it offers. But
you are beginning to see that all it offers is a feeling of the
illusion of safety, better put, a feeling of numbness.
Remember, as was said in the last book, 'You would never
put your life on hold.' Well, buckle up, it is about to get
interesting.*

*What I will be telling you to help you develop these talents
is applicable for everyone. Do not be concerned about
what others might think. Remember you are merely a
messenger. As you have a saying on your planet, 'Don't
shoot the messenger.' The psychic realm covers so much
more than foretelling future events. Actually, someone
with the ability to tell the future but lacks love,
compassion and integrity offers very little to their
brothers and sisters.*

*I will be concerned with having you cultivate certain
attributes so that when these abilities come forth you can
use them in a way that will mirror Honor, Compassion,
and Excitement. You must remember how much you have
an effect on others, as this ability can lend itself to be
abused. Actually, everyone has these abilities, whether
they are psychic or otherwise. These gifts when used for
good can bring forth joy for both participants, and if it
lacks joy in your awareness, you have offered little to the
recipient.*

*Each one of these concepts or tasks I will lay out for you
have the singular purpose of helping you become aware of
your Oneness with everyone and everything. And in the
doing you will experience the overwhelming feeling of
Now or the Totality of Now. This will help you feel the
love that is constantly trying to overlay all your
interactions with others. The deeper you love yourself, the
deeper you will naturally love others. And to love others is
to be one with them, to be one with your Creator.*

With this inner knowing you will naturally know what is going on with another at a thought level, which is really just aligning your vibration with theirs. When you have done this, you will know and feel the Oneness with everyone and everything. Therefore, psychic abilities are really a by-product of being spiritually attuned to who you are as a child of God. I believe that the previous sentence needs repeating. Therefore, psychic abilities are really a by-product of being spiritually attuned to who you are as a child of God.

These exercises will be beneficial for everyone, regardless of whether or not they want to develop their psychic abilities. Psychic abilities are not doled out to certain people but are standard equipment within each of you. Use them wisely and many will be the recipient of these psychic 'gifts.'

The first concept I want you to focus on is your awareness of things and people. You, and the vast majority of your brothers and sisters, really never focus on the subject matter at hand. You have acquired the attribute of multi-tasking and think that has improved your life. Technically, multi-tasking is impossible as in each second your mind can only be in one place at a time, but because of the nature of speed with which you switch from one object to another, you have the illusion of multi-tasking. What I'd like you to do is take specific timeouts each day to actually observe what you are looking at. It might be good to give yourself a test. Look at someone or a particular object, then turn around and describe what you have seen. Be very detailed in your description, and then turn back around and see how well you have done. I believe most will be amazed at how little they actually observe what they are viewing.

There are countless ways to channel someone who no longer has a body. One technique is no better than another. The person you are trying to make contact with is more than willing to meet with you in any format you will allow him or her. If an audible voice would be potentially frightening to you, then they will try another way to get the messages on the other side to you.

Most people find that sleeping dreams are usually the best venue to make contact with those on the other side. When we are asleep we lose identification with the body and ego and are actually in spirit form, just like those on the other side. So for most of you the highest likelihood of making contact with a loved one in your dreams is to set the intention before going to sleep at night. Ask them to be with you and let them know that you have the willingness to remember those interactions from your dreams.

Other ways to make contact includes channel writing, which simply means setting the intention to connect to someone on the other side while writing with a pen and paper or typing on your computer. Just listen within your heart and write down whatever comes to you. We mean write down whatever comes to you. At first, messages will seem irrelevant to you and lack validity to what is occurring in your life. But keep writing and eventually things will start coming to you. It is also important with each interaction to set an intention to speak only with the person you want to contact.

Other ways include meditating on your loved one, an apparition chamber, listening to music that reminds you of your loved one, and listening to the messages attached to those words. Actually, your loved one tries to get messages to you through things we view in everyday life. Look at the clouds, billboards, bumper stickers, and numbers, which all can have meaning.

If you truly want to make contact, the ways are infinite. And if you are trying but are fearful of what might happen, nothing will work. The modality is only as good as your willingness to want to make contact. If there is fear involved, ask your loved one or guardian angel to help you remove those fears

You may also set the intention to connect with your guardian angel to ask questions and receive guidance. Communication with your angels is done in the same fashion as connecting with loved ones. Set your intention to speak with your guardian angels and ask that your messages have a divine source, then proceed to converse in the methodology that works best for you."

Never identify with your doing, but only in your being

Chapter 3: Ego

Identifying with the Body:

"We are still amazed, although We truly shouldn't be how you still identify yourselves as a body. It is like putting on a suit and telling others you are the suit. Or think because you drive a car, therefore you are the car. The more you identify with who you are as a child of God, the body no longer becomes your primary level of reality/focus.

Before We go any further, when Dad wrote, 'We are still amazed,' that was done in a playful manner. On the other side of the veil there is only Love, only Joy, and playfulness is an attribute of our Love that has no beginning and no end. We would highly recommend daily to be playful with yourselves, your bodies, and your loved ones. Remember my words were Honor, Compassion, and Excitement. When you are living your life within those parameters, playfulness will overlay all your interactions. Playfulness is not being foolish but a gentle feeling of laughter that will bring a smile to your face and those with whom you interact. There is never a laughing at, but merely a loving and entertaining observation one might have while observing a precious child. If your playfulness is coming from your egoic thought system, others will feel somehow taken advantage of. When it comes from your ego, then your body will indicate the discord and you will feel uncomfortable. You know the difference. Be that One!

The proper use of the body is accomplished by allowing the body to be a vortex for love. This is accomplished by invoking these two methods: One is the extension of the Love of God to others who still identify themselves as a body. The second is done through the dynamics of forgiveness, which is really nothing more than the removal of your egoic thought system – simply a change of thought. Once again, We are trying to be somewhat playful here because some of these topics will be rather unsettling to most. So when We said, 'which is really nothing more than the removal of your egoic thought system,' that too was done in a playful manner.

I'm sure most have found the removal of one's repressed fears can seem like a monumental task. It can be done by merely asking for assistance and setting the intention to remove all connections to fear within your being. It may take numerous sessions to complete this as you peel back the layers of your fears. (Much like peeling an onion) Once you release one or more fears, then others will float to the surface and will need clearing as well. Just continue to ask for assistance from Anderson, your guardian angels or spirit guides to assist you in this process."

The Egoic Mind:

"The ego is your false self. It is the belief or thought that I am anything other than pure Love. The ego is a word sometimes used interchangeably with the devil and viewed by others as an outside deity fighting against one's heart's desires. There are those that depict the ego as a type of a necessary aspect of oneself that is needed to function in the world. Actually, none of these descriptions accurately depict the creation of the egoic mind, nor its purpose.

The egoic mind is an illusionary aspect of the mind that we think controls our thoughts, words, deeds, and actions. The way we will describe the ego and its function or purpose will sound insane because once you strip the egoic mind to its core beliefs, you will see that it is truly insane. The singular purpose of the egoic mind is to keep you away from Love. Odd as that sounds that is the purpose you give the ego. We need to stress this over and over again: YOU and only you have given it that purpose.

In and of itself, the ego is just performing its duties based on the information it is being fed. It neither loves nor hates you; it simply does what it is told. Like a car, when you put it in drive, it goes forward; when you put it in reverse, it goes back. The car doesn't love you; it is simply doing what you have told it to do.

The first step in understanding this concept is to clearly see exactly what the ego does, where it takes its orders from, and for what purpose. When one understands this concept, each will have to realize that attacking the ego simply will not remove these unwanted feelings. Actually, attacking the ego, making war with the ego, only reinforces the belief that the ego is of value. Attacking the ego is like feeding it. The attack gives justification to the ego's illusionary voice to continue acting out its assigned duties. With this constant feeding it grows in strength and importance. It is only when we stop feeding it does it eventually 'die.' Hopefully, you can see that by making 'attack' a viable option in your mind, the ego and all the pain that comes with it is solidly maintained.

With this newfound knowledge that any attempt to destroy the ego is futile, one must seek a viable option. The next step in slowing down the destruction the ego brings is to give the ego a different job description. Remember, your egoic mind is a computer, what you put into it comes out in different forms. So you must put new information into your mind, and what you now picture from this shift will eventually manifest in your world. The world is neither good nor bad but simply mirrors all your collective thoughts.

A mirror is a good analogy. If one puts an apple in front of the mirror, an apple will show up in the mirror. If the picture of the apple in the mirror engenders fear, then one can simply remove the apple and put something else in place of it. Then assuming the new object is pleasant, the fear will be removed. With the help of the Holy Spirit you can tell your mind 'I want a different result,' and the mind will bring forth those desired results.

But even giving the ego a different role still requires a plethora of on-going conscious decisions. This process is very time consuming and still requires one to endure pain during the transformation process. Let's look at how to remove this painful aspect of our mind. It is still a process, but the removal can be done in a more simplified and gentler methodology.

Because of these energetic shifts that will be coming into the planet, it is imperative that one aligns themselves with their Creator. The fastest way to remove the egoic part of the mind is in one's dreams. We can sum this subject up in one sentence and then expand on the many facets of the egoic mind. The ego is your false self, the self you made, the mask, the persona you wear to keep yourself away from Love.

Why you made your false self is the hardest question to answer, because the answer has to come from outside the egoic mind. Reason, logic, and your intellect all emanate from your egoic mind, so what We are about to set forth will have the egoic mind running amuck with logic and reason to disprove what We said. Your egoic mind will tell you what we are saying is delusional and for you to run away as fast as you can. Why; because these spiritual truths will lead to the end of your ego and it knows that. During the process of really understanding this concept, your ego will likely bring up significant fear from your ego, as it doesn't understand the true Spirit Self.

Be kind, and ask if your egoic mind has brought you the peace you have been pursuing. If so, I'm happy for you.

Put this book down and go forth. But the mere fact that you are reading this book surely has to indicate otherwise. Therefore, please consider that what We are bringing forth is true, internalize as much as you can, and then come back to Us and learn about the bountiful, unlimited Love set before you. Anything new takes time for the mind to absorb, and that may be the case for you with the messages that are being presented. Take the time to work through the acknowledgement of these new concepts.

We will not divide the ego into psychological functions, as a therapist might set forth and attempt to accomplish. We are also not saying whether a therapist's training is correct or incorrect. We are merely looking solely at the motive of your ego. So whether it is the id, ego, or super ego, each has a singular purpose, and that is to keep you away from Love. The egoic mind does this through the only things it can offer you: projection and denial.

The ego's singular goal is to keep you looking outwardly for that illusive love it knows you could never find. But it always holds out hope that there is always another person or item to bring you this peace that can only come through your Creator. It does this to keep you from remembering that you are one with your Creator.

You are one with every living thing in the universe. You are also eternal, and the only emotion you are truly capable of is Love. The ego tells you that you have to earn God's Love, and it gives you a long list of things you have to complete in order to earn God's Love. Funny thing about the ego, even if you do complete its illusionary and insane assignments, it will simply redirect you and start you on another list. There is NO way out of the egoic thought system from within the same delusional thought system that created it in the first place. You must step out of the ego to be able to see all as it really is.

If you listen to your true voice, then you will see the innate offering of your ego. Your Spirit Self will never tell you that you need do anything to become One with your Creator. You are already One. You need do nothing to acquire God's Love. God's Love is always a part of you. You are Love. God is Love, and the only thing that can emanate from God's Love is Love. And since your Creator is constantly extending Herself, this extension is also you. When one comes to the total remembrance of who they are, it will always be accompanied with the realization that there was nothing it ever has to do to attain this state of perfect Love.

What can you do to get out of your ego, given where you believe you are right now? If you believe that you are a body, then give your body and ego a different purpose. Whenever the intent of your thoughts and actions is to help another person, then you are outside of your ego. Whenever you live your life with the purpose of love and serving others, then you are living in Spirit.

Actually, the ego has been described and depicted as something similar to the devil. In fact, it has very similar aspects, except your ego is only a thought and not a person. The devil, if it did exist, would be an outside force fighting for your soul/mind. This imaginary devil force would try to prove how unworthy you are and how bad you are. Then because of the innumerable sinful acts you have committed, you would be required to atone for your transgressions. Even if that was true, which it isn't, within that thought system you could never pay off your karmic debt. In reality, this is how your egoic mind makes you feel and act, as if you are anything but love. How hopeless and very unnecessary all these egoic thoughts are to you.

So once again, We will state it over and over again. The reason We do so is because you have to see the insanity of the offerings of your egoic mind before you will make another choice. So be kind to yourself. One could lose *themselves in all the guilt they carry around believing they have committed sins in the past. There is no sin that your **Spirit** has committed as it is incapable of committing sin. All your body has ever done is made mistakes while living your human existence. Let the Voice for Truth become your cosmic eraser and banish these thoughts from the most holy mind that God created within you. Whenever you find yourself living through your ego, choose again. With each action you perform ask yourself: 'How can I perform this action coming from love?' Stop and reflect on this a moment and the answer will come to you, and then you will know what to do. Make this a daily practice and soon it will become how you live each moment."*

The Veil and Separate Realities:

"In between the two apparent but seemingly separate realities of your Spirit and ego is what appears to be a vaporous sphere that separates the two worlds. This vaporous sphere lies between the seen and the unseen. Some spiritual thought systems refer to this seemingly divisive layer as a veil, in addition to other various names. Between the seen and the unseen there is a side that gives rise to an apparent reality because of the five senses, and there is the other side which projects an energetic level where the 'dead' seem to reside.

Much has been written about the other side, but not about what seems to separate the denser vibrational frequencies that projects itself into form and the higher vibrational frequencies that cannot normally be seen nor felt on this side of the veil. Each of these energetic frequencies, the seen or unseen, can never come together because of their different modulations. So We will not ask why the seen and the unseen cannot merge but, 'Why the veil and its purpose?'

In answering the question of the veil, one should be aware that it is a self-imposed barrier. This veil is put there by your ego as a defense mechanism against your true Spirit Self or God. You see, your ego believes that once you are one with God, there is no longer a need for your body. The ego is fearful that you will lay your body down once you have reached this level of enlightenment. In reality, it is at this point that you are ready to assume your purpose for being here.

On this side of the veil you have emotions of shame, guilt, and unworthiness, just to name a few. And it is because of these lower frequency emotions that the veil gets projected outwardly. In projecting these emotions outward towards someone or something else, your ego doesn't have to deal with why you should feel this way. If the negative emotions are given an outside cause, then you don't have to own them. Again, all this is done by the ego with the singular purpose of keeping yourself away from your Source. Again, it does this because it believes that if you are deemed guilty of these acts, then you will eventually be condemned by God.

Remember, any thought that is not in alignment with your higher Self will eventually have to produce thoughts of guilt, shame or unworthiness. It is because of these beliefs that we have done something bad we feel we have to punish ourselves. Of course, none of this is true, but it makes little difference to the egoic mind. The egoic mind has built its own internal veil, and it is called 'projection.' Now, within that mindset of, 'I'm a bad person,' we then feel unworthy. This misplaced guilt is the root cause of everyone feeling unworthy of God's Love. And so now we have created a God that has some emotion other than Love. In reality that is impossible, but within our unworthiness we cannot conceive of a God being unlike ourselves.

I am sure most of you have read in the Bible that God created you in His image. Now, through your projections, the ego mind returns the favor and creates a God in your image. This made-up god is now capable of judgment, because that is an egoic thought. Then because of this judgment we need a place to hide from god. Why; because we believe he has to punish us for our transgressions. Remember, we now have created a god like us. Thus, the veil is made in the mistaken belief that it can protect us by keeping a wrathful god at bay. Such foolishness is given to these thoughts. As insane as this paragraph might sound, that is what is taking place within the insanity of the egoic mind.

Once you give your life a different purpose, this illusionary veil will vanish into the nothingness from which it was made. In giving your life's purpose the extension of Love, your channel to those on the other side will open up. Why; because whenever your energy is in alignment with Love, you are modulating at the same frequency as those on the other side. Since those on the other side are always in the frequency of Love, you will be transmitting and receiving on the same level, and there will be no barriers between the two worlds."

Projection:

Projection is the process of trying to get rid of something undesirable, usually a repressed issue. This is done through the process of throwing the undesirable thought onto someone or something else. This is impossible and only reinforces the issue within the mind of the one trying to magically dispose of their repressed fears. We laugh on this side of the veil at how you feel projection can actually be accomplished. You feel this apparatus you call a body can actually see, feel, smell, and dictate to you what emotions you should have based on the erroneous feedback the ego has given you.

What actually takes place is you, your mind, looks inside and is left with only two options. Oh, you think you have numerous ones, but there are only two. If you decide to listen to the voice of your ego and what the ego has to offer, then that is all you can see and witness. If you look inside and determine the Voice for Truth has more to offer you, then a completely different world will open up before you. Oh, your eyes will see the same things, but your interpretation of all that is around you will be completely different.

Once again, technically speaking, projection is impossible. Projection basically states that whatever lies inside one's mind and is considered undesirable can be erased by throwing it onto someone or something else. When you really look at it, you will have to see the insanity of such a silly technique.

Projection has become the substitute of your true vision. Vision is seeing your world through the eyes of God and thus being One with what you see. With this love in your heart, your eyes gather different information, and, therefore, your responses have to be different. You are here to usher in a new world, and the only way you can begin this process is by seeing the new world first within your mind. This is only accomplished by giving what you are presently witnessing a divine purpose. Now you are ready to usher in a new world."

The Pain of Separation:

"Pain is such a great motivator. You have trained yourself to learn though pain. We are not saying one shouldn't learn through pain, but there are definitely

*better, gentler methods at your disposal. Pain indicates
something has gone amiss, and that is true. But your egoic
mind believes what has gone amiss was caused by
something external. This pain, caused by an external
event, then causes you an emotion of something other than
love. With that erroneous thought one must seek to solve
the problem externally.*

*But with this new energy coming into your planet, there
will be a different type or a higher vibration of disconnect
for those not in alignment with their higher Self. This type
of disconnect has never been felt before on your planet,
and this disconnect can no longer be denied. It is intended
that way – this pain of disconnection from your source
will motivate you to change. Actually, we have trouble
using the word 'pain' because actually it is just an
emotion other than Love. And any emotion other than
Love, if given its rightful purpose, has the singular
purpose of motivating you back towards Love. What We
are trying to do here is to entice you into being motivated
through Love rather than fear."*

Good nor bad exist

except in the name

Chapter 4: Fear

Manifesting:

"Manifesting seems to be a new phenomenon on your planet, like someone just came up with it. Manifesting has always been in existence since thought was first introduced. And there has never been a time when there has been an absence of thought. From a practical perspective, and we need to keep it that way, the best way to explain manifesting is to start by saying it is impossible not to manifest. Every thought produces something on your viewing screen, which is just another word for world. Therefore, the world is neither good nor bad, but simply mirrors back the thoughts you have placed onto your screen as your definition and interpretation of the world you see.

You can't stop manifesting because the mind is never void of thought, but you can change what you are manifesting by changing your thoughts. So if you don't like what is occurring in your life and your subsequent feelings, simply change your thoughts about that subject, person or thing. Sounds simple I know, but the application of this concept is the hardest part.

There has to be a reason to change what one is thinking, and this is where feelings are so important. Your feeling nature is the singular indicator as to which voice you are listening to. If what you see is bringing you an emotion other than pure love, you are listening to the ego. If what you are seeing is bringing you joy, then you are listening to the Voice for Truth. It really boils down to something that simple. Really it IS that simple. You can't deny how you feel, and trying to bury your feelings only makes the pain worse when it is finally brought back into your conscious mind.

View all that you see through love and you will manifest love back within your life. As you act from love you will vibrate at the energy level of love. This will allow you to fully connect with those on the other side of the veil and to know what your purpose and path is for this lifetime. This love will carry you through each day and continue to manifest abundance for you. Remember a kaleidoscope is to remind you of your option to choose again. You merely need to shift your view ever so slightly to see all as it really is."

The Effects of Fear:

"The fact that We are using the word 'effects' should indicate to you that there must be a 'cause' from somewhere. What is the cause of fear? The cause of fear is your egoic thoughts. It is only at the frequency of the egoic mind where fear can be seen and thus ultimately felt. All thoughts emanating from the egoic mind will eventually produce the effects of fear, because the egoic mind knows not of love.

The illusion that fear holds out is that some of the effects that are produced by the egoic mind can also be labeled as good. The ego is a genius at devising ways to keep you from recognizing who you are. Fears come from the inability to understand who you really are. What the ego categorizes as good is what it can store away in the subconscious mind without the possibility of resurfacing. What is bad is what it is unable to repress. The ego labels and names everything and likes to study what it has made. To the ego the Totality of Now is but an illusionary story told by those unwilling to face 'reality.' That way it keeps you from questioning its own processes.

Be kind to yourself in dealing with the effects of fear. Start where the fear originates, which is really nothing more than a thought in your mind projected outwardly. Take sole responsibility for your emotions, and then you will be in control of your life. Your thoughts are the only thing you do have control of in your life. You may have the illusionary thought of 'If I can rearrange everything external to me that cause pain, then I will be happy.' What a daunting task to undertake and, We might add, an impossible task even for the grandiosity of your ego.

It is only through listening to your Voice for Truth and asking to see your true gifts behind the fear that one can start on the most joyous journey undertaken on your planet. Be that One that says 'Yes' to God!"

Guilt:

"You have two diametrically opposing thought systems at your disposal at all times. These two thought systems are your egoic mind and your spirit mind. Both your spiritual messages and physical sensory inputs are coming into your mind at once. How you interpret them and the consequences of your interpretations are all being played out constantly in your mind. Both types of these messages are beings transmitted even during your sleeping state, but you can't hear them both simultaneously because your mind can only be at one vibrational frequency at a time. It is like tuning a radio. You can't hear AM and FM at the same time; you must choose which channel and frequency you want to hear.

When listening to your egoic voice, it will always tell you that you are guilty. You can never do enough, give enough, nor atone enough to hear a not-guilty verdict. Oh, it dresses up what you have done or what you have

41

*said in an effort to make you feel good temporarily, but
the underlining message is always the same - guilty as
charged. I know you don't like to hear this and you feel
the ego does offer you hope and is good in certain areas.
We have to say, 'No, it really doesn't offer any true hope,
but it does hold out the illusion of hope.' This hope lies
solely in an external search for love, which is always
outside you. As long as you search outside of yourself for
love you will never find it.*

*Your ego has caused you to become addicted to seeking
love. You even have the illusion of feeling you are getting
better at searching. We laugh, with Love I might add, at
the enormous effort you put forth in seeking outwardly
what cannot be found. You judge others by their ability to
overcome obstacles; you even call them heroes. You even
seem at times to worship those that have overcome
obstacles. But the hope lies in searching externally for
what can only be found internally. The reason you look
outside yourself can only come from the fear of looking
within. Looking inward to overcome obstacles is what will
bring success.*

*And because you have become addicted to searching for
love, there seems to be that elusive hope of another
search, another book, another person or substance which
can be found that will finally end this discomfort each of
you carry. But, once again, as long as the search is
external, and it must be as long as you listen to this egoic
voice of madness, pain will eventually be felt. You can
only search externally for so long before many will make
the conscious choice to numb themselves to keep the pain
of failure at bay.*

*Our ego cries out, although subconsciously, 'There are
others that are more deserving of god's wrath than
myself.' It is then that our old friend 'projection' comes
into play and your mind tells each of you that you are
good, and the other people are the bad ones. Be honest,*

don't each of you feel like you are good, and there are other people outside of you who are much more deserving of god's wrath? Everyone feels justified in what they do and believe, and then they judge the world according to their beliefs.

But, hopefully, you have come to notice one common characteristic after each search, regardless of whether you have reached your goal or not. If you are looking anywhere else for love other than from within, then you will still end up with a feeling other than love. Your feelings of emptiness, shame, and unworthiness all encompass the egoic mind, and from within that frequency there is no way out.

Sometimes you may not feel the 'unworthy' grip on your mind, because you have accomplished an egoic goal. This 'victory' does feel good momentarily because your fears have been repressed, but because of your false belief in a wrathful god, your 'unworthy' feelings will need to reemerge once again. These feelings will usually occur with a little more intensity wrapped around an illusionary offering of peace/love/joy. So off you go on another search, always feeling that this time it will be different. Hope is inevitable, but you must place your hope in a different place other than on these false idols you have made as replacements for your true source of joy.

The ego's search is virtually endless. It seems never to run out of options. One must finally come to the realization that this searching is all in vain and will not bring you the inner peace your heart is so desperately crying out for. It is only when you can begin an internal quest where the outcome is now certain. You will be at peace here because once the journey has started the end is certain.

Let your body and your emotions be your guide. Any emotion you are feeling that isn't in pure alignment with love and joy will eventually bring on a guilty feeling as a by-product of any of these other emotions. Whenever guilt finally comes into your awareness you will end up feeling bad and unworthy. And, once again, that is when your ego will come to your rescue. It rides up like a knight on a white horse to save you from your guilt. It projects this guilt onto someone else thereby releasing you of your guilt. And through this projection it offers the illusion of hope that you have been saved from your wrathful God. You will follow your ego's instructions because of the deep desire to eradicate these feelings of guilt and fear. Instead of listening to the ego, you should seek your Spirit Self, and then request its assistance to release all thoughts associated with God being anything other than love.

The ego deals with guilt in other ways as well. The ego, never wanting you to look inwardly, tells you that by punishing yourself you can remove these unwanted feelings. Since you feel you have no other alternative, you start on the painful course of punishing yourself in the mistaken belief that it will remove the undesirable guilty thoughts and associated fear.

Another process in the ego's arsenal for removing these unwanted guilty thoughts is to figure out how bad you really were. The ego literally weighs everything. And from this seemingly quantitative weight of guilt you will seek out ways to atone for your transgressions. This atonement will be in the exact proportion to the guilt you have assigned your bad deed. And from this process the ego is always making a judgment of one's self-worth.

Your ego believes that once you have 'paid off' your transgression and your time for the crime has been served, then you are released from your crimes. Now it tells you your punishment is served, and the ego's version of god will now welcome you back with open arms. The best you can hope for is a furlough for your misdeeds. Within this thought system the ego always keeps a record of your crimes. And with the next mistake you make, it will

*simply add that to your present record. Hopefully, you can
see that by truly undressing what is really taking place
within the egoic thought system, you would have to
conclude that this atoning process is insane. With that in
mind, now the mind has another option. Let us look at the
only one true alternative to the ego's many offerings. Now
is the time to remind the ego that God is Love and as such
can only give you love."*

Deflecting Guilt:

*"Notice how the title is stated – 'deflecting guilt.' What
We are trying to present to you is a method upon which
you will leave guilt with no place to land. Guilt needs a
place for it to be nurtured, or it will dissolve into the
nothingness from which it came. Guilt is solely a product
of the egoic mind. This guilt your mind now perceives was
made from a fearful thought. The result of each fearful
thought is an accompanying thought of guilt. The main
aspect of guilt is that it demands punishment for all those
involved, and, yes, that includes you.*

*Guilt can only survive in a setting that is conducive to
maintaining the original feeling from which it was
birthed. If one blames another person, the world, or some
other event, rather than taking full responsibility for its
birthing, one is furnishing guilt with the food it needs to
grow and fester. To really alleviate this guilt one must
first look within to realize they are the creator of every
emotion that produced the feelings of guilt in the first
place. It is then that one can begin the forgiveness
process. This self-forgiveness causes guilt to be deflected
because it now has no place to land."*

Being Worthy:

"If one measures their self-worth by what one has accumulated, one will always feel less than. The egoic mind lives by comparisons, and there will always be someone bigger, better, and has acquired more than you. Within the framework of the egoic mind you can never have enough, do enough, or be enough to feel worthy. You are NOT a miserable sinner. You are perfect right where you are. You were created by Love, and this Love knows no limits. It's only desire for you is joy and happiness.

Your Spirit Self knows the only way one can ever feel worthy is in the doing of what you are guided to do in that moment. By listening to the Divine Voice, one cannot fail because then you will be in alignment with the natural order of things on this planet. Failure can only be experienced when one has set out to accomplish something that is not in alignment with the Voice for Truth. It is that pursuit to achieve egoic goals that takes you away from who you are as a child of God. This constant outward seeking ultimately produces an emotion of failure. But by merely shifting the purpose of what you are doing and then by giving it a divine purpose, one can only feel worthy as a result. In giving each of your interactions a divine purpose, a strong sense of worth will overlay not only what you are doing but also your emotions attached to the doing."

Chapter 5: Our Relationship with Time

Time:

"The aspect of viewing time is solely undertaken by the egoic mind. The egoic mind is the only place that time has any meaning. You experience time coming from your dualist thought system. You view it in a linear fashion, seeing the sequence of past, present, and future. Your mind unfolds a future like your past, and, thus, one just 'marks' time.

Within this thought process there is no way to experience a true now. You are always thinking from a past perspective and overlay your interpretation of the past over your current viewing screen. Therefore, what you see is determined by your past thoughts and your future will merely be a repeat of your past thoughts.

To view how time really is being played out, one must come from a completely different thought process. No matter how We present these new perspective messages words can be inadequate. The reason for that is your egoic mind tries to understand these new concepts, and when it can't, it then attaches past symbols to new words, making concrete symbols for each new thought that crosses its mind. Your egoic mind runs amuck with words as Oneness, Divine Love, Infinite, God, etc., because it has trouble picturing a symbol it can attach to these words. This particular subject, as well as numerous other spiritual concepts, can only be experienced in the Now without translation from the ego.

Thus, the reason for trying to explain topics like what the new world will look like can be rather perplexing. The new world will take form resulting from feelings of love. The egoic mind knows not of love but does know how to picture things, take orders from a manual, and follow instructions. So it needs something that it can see, feel, and touch because that is all it knows. It knows not of your heart's desires.

All of time is really wrapped up in one instant. In this instant, within the conception of the ego, is actually the birthing of time. Time is of a single instant but keeps getting repeated, like an endless loop, over and over. Each thought of time mirrors some aspect of the original thought of separation, although it appears to move forward.

What We are asking you to do is step out of time, while being in time. That is not as difficult as you might think. Time's singular purpose is to keep you from being in the Now. Therefore, the undoing of time is accomplished by giving time a different purpose. In doing this with each interaction, you will eventually come to a place where love overlaps each thought, and you can actually live in the Now.

To practice stepping out of time, ask yourself this question, "How can I see my brothers and sisters as they were created by God?" In doing this, you allow your Creator to paint a picture on a blank canvas. To the degree of sincerity in the asking of the above question, one can have a present thought about the past without a contrasting thought. Think on that awhile!

Remember, to create a thought within the ego framework requires a contrasting view of the objects. When one solely listens to the Voice for Truth, you will have numerous thoughts but they are all the same – they are Love. So from that perspective you will go through life in

*a continuous NOW state. Therefore, you are in time but
not ruled by time. Be that One!"*

Bi-Location:

*"Hopefully, one can at least intellectually understand the
concept of time. When one is able to step out of time,
within the frequency of the world as you now experience
it, one can start to understand how one can be in two
places at the same time. If everything is the result of a
thought, which it is, that single thought can be everywhere
at once. That is why you can still communicate with those
on the other side. Oh, don't say you haven't tried.
Everyone has asked for help from some deity that is void
of a bodily form.*

*Everyone bi-locates each day, whether or not they know
when it occurs. If you go to sleep, you are bi-locating;
your body is one place, and your mind is somewhere else.
The first obstacle to bi-location that one must overcome is
defining which 'you' We are referring to. You are not a
body. The body is not who you are; your scientist have
proven that to be true. Also, you believe that there is a
part of you that goes on when the body is laid down. The
part of you that continues is who you really are and that
has never died.*

*In focusing on the real you, whether you call it your spirit,
soul or some other name, that essence of you is energy. In
fact, it is Divine energy that is continuously evolving
deeper and deeper into the Love of God. If that energy is
everywhere, which it is, then this energy can take its form
in more than one place."*

Our Relationship to Time:

"First, let's look at time. The people on planet Earth, which I now so lovingly call 'my brothers and sisters,' perceive time in a linear fashion. In reality, time is only/all happening in the NOW. In fact, a better way to state it would be to say it is all happening in a continuous NOW.

I will do the best I can to explain the concept that time is all occurring now. For many this concept will be difficult to comprehend. Your ego thought processes cannot grasp this because it cannot rationally explain how that could occur. In order to understand the concept, you will need to picture all of time as being a single instant in eternity. Next, you will need to picture that singular instant being divided and subdivided over and over again until you have reached a number that is inconceivable. That is what you have done with eternity, and now you must view this concept of time from these tiny fragments.

Time is one of the more difficult concepts to bring forth because you identify with your body and with living in a world where everything has a beginning and an end. In between a beginning and an end, there is a point A and a point B. The result of thinking you are separate beings gives rise to the illusion of time, and with that illusion one becomes a slave to time and space. That is why bodies and things become old and wear out.

Because we label things and people everything will eventually have to disintegrate. Nothing conceived within time will last forever because it was born in time. Time wears out everything because of the constant judgment that is overlaid on each object or person one views on their screen. The laying aside of judgment is impossible within the concept of time.

Notice how in the above paragraph We stated, 'Time wears out everything because of the constant judgment that is overlaid on each object or person one views on their screen.' Judgment is only part of YOUR world. Your judgment is always associated with condemnation because when one chooses one thing over another, one must also include in their judgment what they have judged against. It is this judgment that wears everything out within this world. This usually isn't done consciously because most judgments take place on what you would call 'mundane' issues.

Therefore, when one is ready, even within the concept of a body and mind, one is capable of stepping out of time. This is accomplished when one listens to the Voice for God. In this listening, you are actually in a state of timelessness because you are not judging what you see. Now, you have given the body a divine purpose and have risen above the laws of karma. Ask to give your mundane tasks a divine purpose - eating, reading the paper, watching TV, etc. In giving what you do a divine purpose; you can temporarily step into your ultimate purpose of being a co-creator with God. That is giving the body its ultimate purpose of Love.

Time appears and is talked about as if it happens in a linear fashion. You have a past, present, and an anticipated future, and in between these three aspects duration of time exists. From your perception, time exists within your typical vibrational frequency. But in the vibrational frequency of Love, time does not exist. And since you are love, at the core of your being you are never tied to time or the effects of time. There are steps you can take that will help you transcend from a time-based reality to living amongst your brothers and sisters in a timelessness state. You can accomplish this 'timelessness' process within the world of time by giving your body and thoughts a divine purpose. Be that One!"

Time is Now:

"Once again, time is probably one of the hardest things to explain because We are trying to explain infinity using a finite language. The egoic mind is based in time. It is based on a point A and a point B, and the requirement for an interval of time in going from point A to point B.

What most of you are unaware of is that every possible event that anyone on your planet could ever have come up with within the frequency of time is written within the minds of all. In that one instant of time you believe you are separated from the Totality of Now. That is the origin of guilt and the birthing of time. For every egoic fear that you have brought into your most holy mind, the origin can be traced back to the original cause of not knowing who you really are. Scientists have called this thought of separateness the 'Big Bang Theory' – which is what caused the creation of your solar system. This is when the One created the many from itself.

Once you deemed yourself separate, then a new reality or universe had to be invented to explain this separateness. The creation of this universe occurred with the birth of time and is all part of the egoic thought system. It is important to understand that none of this changes who you really are. You are Oneness!

Whenever one of my brothers or sisters has a thought within this frequency of time, it gets projected outwardly. Each of you has the innate ability to tap into those projected thoughts. You can either choose between knowing and not knowing what another person is thinking. Most of you are completely unaware you have this ability, so your choice becomes an automatic 'not knowing.'

Please be aware that once you can tap into a projected thought, that doesn't mean you need to believe it. It simply means the thought and whatever it holds is available to all who are open to hearing. It would be like someone believing the world is flat. That doesn't mean everyone else has to attach themselves to that particular belief. But that thought is still out there, and if one's vibrational frequency is similar, one will be aware of the thought that was projected from another.

But what one has to see is that every possible event that anyone could have dreamed of within your concept of past, present and future time has already happened. I know that is difficult to understand, but think of your radio waves – you are listening to one station and cannot possibly conceive of another station being played at the same time. In reality, they are all being played at one time, but because you can only be attuned into one frequency at any given moment, you can only hear what is available to be heard at that frequency. Classical music stations, country, rock, easy listening, etc., are all playing at the same time, and we have the choice of which one we will listen to at any given moment. It would be like someone listening to a country music station from 9am to 10am, while someone else is listening to a rock station from 9am to 10am, and the one listening to the country music station thinks the other person is crazy because only country music was being played at that time."

Collapsing Time:

"Look at your life like you are viewing a movie and each scene is a segment in your mind that gets projected onto your viewing screen/world. You have an enormous amount of segments each day. Segments can be used interchangeable with thought. Each separate thought is within the vibrational frequency of the egoic mind. The collapse of time is the removal of all these different contrasting thoughts.

When your singular focus is purely on extending love, time, in the sense that you now experience it, disappears, and you live in what is known as a 'thoughtlessness' state. Thoughtlessness is not the absence of thought but the absence of contrasting thoughts. You currently live in a word of duality and contrast, good/bad, right/wrong, male/female, hot/cold, etc. When one gives up the need to be right or to be special, the egoic mind disappears into the nothingness of the illusionary vapor from which it was made. Now that you know this, your new role and singular purpose will be to help others remember who they are.

In this frequency of Love, the joy that you will experience is indescribable. Words cannot describe what We speak of. In using words to describe something or someone, your mind has to have a picture or, at the very least, a symbol to attach as meaning or the word is meaningless. In the frequency of Love, you are not dealing with a person or a thing but a feeling. The joy that you will experience is literally not of this world. It cannot be described because we are speaking of a feeling of Love that has no known parallel in which you can compare.

From a purely spiritual perspective, every thought at its core has only one purpose, and that is the collapse of time. When this collapse of time occurs, you will all be in the NOW frequency. There will no longer be segments of time or frequencies but a continuous feeling or thought of love. But to begin that process of Oneness, which is what the Now frequency is, one has to give time a different purpose. There I go using the word 'purpose' again, because that is the key to everything on your planet, and time is no exception. When you give time a divine purpose of Love and the intent of bringing all beings back to Oneness, then time will collapse."

Chapter 6: Cause and Effect

Cause and Effect:

"Cause and effect is the most basic and misunderstood principle on your planet. I know that will raise some eyebrows amongst my brothers and sisters, but with your smile accompanies a smile on this side of the veil as well. Why; because it is how you believe the world operates. You describe it as an undeniable law. It is the law which you also believe governs each interaction and relationship, not only between one another, but also between you and inanimate objects and events. This belief permeates all facets of your existence. This is true only when you look at yourself as tied to a body.

As a body you define your relationships with others and inanimate objects as being reciprocal. When We are referring to relationships in this particular context, We are not strictly referring to romantic relationships but also parent/child, siblings, friends, events, and, as We have mentioned before, inanimate objects. If you think you don't have relationships with objects, watch the next time one of them breaks down. Easy to lose your peace, is it not?

True cause and effect is content and form, giving and receiving, God and God's creations. Because you believe you live within a world of contrast, you will experience a cause, and the reaction to that cause comes in the form of some perceived effect. For you, there will be a duration of time between the thought and the effect. This is because you believe you live in a world of time and space, and because of this illusionary state, there will be a time lapse. On a spiritual level, the effect happens at once because in actuality they are inseparable.

We observe your 'effect' on this side of the veil as an emotional charge that you choose in reaction to the perceived cause. You ascribe various names to your 'effect.' For every cause there is an effect, and for every effect there is also a cause. They interlock with each other. What We are trying to show you is you are the cause and what you choose to view in the world and your brothers and sisters are the effect.

You have your normal way of speaking, and how you interact with others is reversed. You see the world and your brothers and sisters as the cause, and you and your emotional response to them as the effect. This naturally leads to various emotions other than love. We are trying to get you to align cause and effect in the way your Creator designed them to unfold on your planet.

At the highest vibrational level, cause and effect cease to exist as separate states. This Oneness, this all-inclusive state, is beyond what one can comprehend within the framework of the egoic mind. But this Oneness is the reason you can never be separate from your Source. This knowledge can only be experienced; it cannot be taught.

If there are no accidents, which is true, and if we are the cause and the world is the effect, which is also true – and there are no exceptions to this – then once there is a cause there also has to be an effect. That's the law! Spiritual Laws have no exceptions, and that is what makes them a law. The law of gravity has no exception. All other Earthly laws have no exceptions, and Spiritual laws have no exception either. Earthly and spiritual laws need neither your belief nor your approval of them for them to work in your life.

Therefore, you are the captain of your ship, your world, and the people in your world. Why; because of the law of cause and effect. You are the cause, and the world the effect. That is exactly opposite to the way most people walk through life. They walk around reacting to the world's stimulus of people and events. Because of this you have allowed the world to be the cause, and you the effect. Do you not see this?

You look inside, which means you look in your mind, determine what your beliefs are about that person or thing, and then project those thoughts outwardly. If you believe the world to be untrustworthy, then all you see will be untrustworthy people and acts because that is what you are looking for. But if you believe all people are love and all their acts are either love or a cry out for love then you will see love in everything.

This outward projection of your thoughts will attract certain people who will mirror your thoughts. When you do this your ego now has someone else to blame for the fear that secretly hides behind the veil your projection overlays within your mind. You have to have someone to blame. Your ego screams frantically in the hope you will reverse your course from looking inward.

We ask you to choose again. Now is the time to remember you are the cause and the world mirrors an effect. Once love is the cause of everything within your mind, then and only then will you be in charge of your destiny."

Give to Receive:

"Notice how the heading reads, 'Give to receive.' It does not read, 'Give and receive.' So We will focus on being consciously awake when giving so one can know what one will be receiving. The ultimate cost of giving something is that you will have to receive the same thing back. That is the law. Start looking at what you have in your life, including the people in your life, and then look at how you interact with those in your life and ask yourself, 'Are you

happy?' If the answer is no, then you need to 'give' what you want in your life. That is exactly 180 degrees opposite to the ego's thought system.

Remember, the ego is maintained and flourished through the dynamics of projection. It gives to get rid of. Hopefully, what will make this law attractive to you is the knowledge that what you are receiving back from what you give is multiplied tens of thousands of times in flow back to you– not just tenfold. So ask yourself before you give something, 'Is this what I want coming back to me?' If not, then refrain from giving it because it is coming back to you in mass quantities.

If you want love in your life, then you are going to have to give it. If you want divine relationships, then you are going to have to be divine. When you remember who you are as a child of God, then you will know that you cannot give away anything but love. And by virtue of our Spiritual Law, the world will return to you more love than you can possibly dream of at the present time. It is important to remember that to truly give love means to give love unconditionally. Your intent is as important as the gift of love itself.

In working with the Spiritual Law of giving and receiving, the receiving of what is being offer doesn't necessarily have to come from the one with whom you have offered something. But it must come back in a form at least as good as it was given – or much more. That is the law!

Reciprocal relationships are truly not relationships. They are a type of partnership in which each person decides on how much they are willing to give the other person in order to get what they want in return. Also, in the giving, one tries to figure out how much one needs to give to get the desired result they are looking for. Giving now has become a source of fear because of the uncertainty of the perceived repayment. This permeates all areas of giving and receiving on your planet.

Now is the time to be honest with yourself in looking at your interactions with others and your Creator. When you interact with others through your ego, ultimately all your relationships will eventually foster disharmony. That is because their source has come from a place of lack and fear and not from love. It is enjoyable watching our Earth-bound brothers and sisters with their interactions with others while they still perceive themselves in a body. Your interactions and how you view others never deviates from how you view yourself. It is impossible to do otherwise because you are the cause of everyone. All the world does is merely mirror back your thoughts projected outwardly."

The Mirror Principle:

"The mirror principle really isn't a principle but a law, but We must tell you it is a law that is overlaid with error. Basically, the way the law works is that 'If you spot it, you got it.' That is true, but not in the way that you might think of it. You interpret this law to mean that if I see a person who is aggressive that must mean I am aggressive. That's not necessarily the case. Once again, you are viewing an internal aspect of yourself externally, and your interpretation will always be wrong.

Remember, the ego never looks inside. This is a secret vow it has kept since its conception. From the perspective of this false self, everything that irritates you is outside of you. What is really taking place on your viewing screen is merely the world mirroring back to you what you believe to be true about yourself. You just don't necessarily know that about yourself. If an egoic thought emanated from the false self, you will naturally see something that produces

59

*an emotion other than love. If it emanates from the Voice
for Truth, our loving Self, what we see externally will also
mirror that belief we hold about our self.*

*Therefore, the world is neither good nor bad but simply
shows us which voice we are hearing. If we see a world of
hatred, our mind is in the grips of the false self. If we see
a world of love, hope, and compassion, the world is just
mirroring back the love, hope and compassion from
within. If the mirror principle is true, which it is because
it is a law, then what you see, what you feel, is the effect
of your thoughts. Thus how you view the world and the
events that take place on your planet will come forth
through your filtering screen, better known as your mind.*

*The egoic mind needs to be understood as a receiving
device that gathers information, and this information is
stored in a memory bank, and this memory bank
determines how it will react to events that are on its
viewing screen. The plethora of information stored in this
memory bank is literally staggering. According to the
dominant information you have put in your memory bank,
it sets forth in motion how you will view the world, and,
ultimately, how you will react to external stimulus that
naturally calls forth a response.*

*To understand why we chose to observe things a certain
way or why you do things, let's take a closer look at why
we store certain beliefs and choose to discard others. I'm
sure you have noticed how different people can view the
same event and give diametrically opposing views of what
just occurred. That is because each person is viewing
what occurred through their egoic filter, which compares
what occurred to what it knows from past experiences.
The ego then 'judges' or 'assumes' what just occurred as
being similar or different to what it knows from the past
and then assigns emotions to it as well. It literally makes
up a story about what just occurred and then believes the
story to be fact.*

The vast majority of concepts or beliefs you hold about yourself and the world are insane. (Sorry. There is no easy way to put this but to say they are insane.) The word 'insane' might seem like a rather strong word to describe how one looks at oneself and others, but it is a perfect way to depict these concepts we hold dear to our hearts. After all, the concepts the ego chooses to believe and store are clearly insane once one sees them for what they are. That is one of the reasons for writing this book, to show the reader the insanity of the egoic thought system, but, more importantly, my purpose is to give you a truly loving alternative. One that can provide you with the peace you so desperately seek.

The insanity of the egoic mind can be easily disapproved if one starts to question the concept of cause and effect. Of all the topics that will be discussed in this book, the ones on the body, energy, and cause and effect, are of imperative importance. The importance of understanding these concepts will help you understand not only how you view yourself, but also how you perceive everyone around you.

Whatever your concepts are of yourself, the ego will project these concepts outwardly, and they will seem true to the perceiver. Therefore, whatever emanates outwardly is a result of what is believed inwardly and will appear to be logical. Logic does not make things true; it simply makes them logical. So if someone has a completely different view of something, it will be hard to argue your point because, in their world, they will attract events to prove their thoughts correct.

The first premise of egoic cause and effect truly has to be questioned at the core level. Hopefully, you can see clearly it is not cause and effect, but effect and cause. In your egoic reality you have external stimuli to which you then react. This external event has become your egoic 'cause' to your emotional state, and now you have become the 'effect.'

Dissolving Cause and Effect:

"So we must first realize 'I am the cause.' Know that each thought that you have is projected into the world as the cause. The effect is the manifestation of each of those thoughts within the world. The world is merely an external mirror or picture of your internal thought. As you subconsciously look inside and determine what you want to experience, you then proceed to manifest matching events to make sure your thought system is right. And in response to your projection, the world will prove your thought system right every time.

As I have previously stated, you really can't get very far arguing with another person's thought system, but you can ask them, 'Does this belief bring you peace?' If their answer is 'No,' then, hopefully, they can change their thoughts, which in turn will change their way of looking at the world, which will manifest a change in their world.

If one can understand they are the cause and the world and people are the effect, now you are in charge of how you view external things, and now you have dominance over your emotions. Once you 'choose again' you cease to be a reaction to these external happenings. This is the most basic law, but also the most freeing law, because it puts you in charge of your life. Why; because you are the cause. But to accept this concept one must no longer blame the world or other people for any events that appear on their screen. Remember, it is your dualistic perceptual viewing screen, and nothing gets on the screen unless it first appeared within your mind. Be grateful for this knowledge because it truly is the dawn of your new awakening.

We are not saying what you saw didn't happen, it did. But what We are saying is you have complete control over your emotional reaction associated with the event. And, now, hopefully, you can choose to put yourself in charge of your thoughts and come from a place of love instead of fear. This coming from a place of love will naturally produce love on your viewing screen.

But there is another level to cause and effect. When one truly understands the total connection to God, cause and effect will no longer exist. Once cause and effect cease to exist to you, you become one with everything. That is when you will come to the realization that there is literally nothing outside of you. Be that One!"

You are the cause
not the effect

Chapter 7: The True Self

God:

This is one of the questions I asked Anderson to explain to me. He had previous spoken to me about deities, and I requested further explanation. Below is his response.

"There isn't a singular God but a cluster of Gods or deities. Dad, the concept of God has evolved over the centuries because the concept of the individual has evolved. You – and when I say 'you,' I am speaking for just about everyone on planet Earth – have great difficulty conceptualizing your Creator unlike yourself.

Your planet is based on a hierarchy system. You have a lower or lesser order in every system. You have a middle category where you insert things based upon importance as you define importance, and, conversely, a higher order reserved for those of ultimate authority or importance. And the higher the order, the more authority appointed to that particular group, or in the majority of cases, a singular person or department. And at the highest level you have the ultimate authority, or what you might refer to as 'the one with the veto power.'

God is one of the more difficult concepts to bring forth to your planet. There are two main reasons for the previous sentence – your belief in a hierarchy in power and your firm belief in a singular way of receiving Love. If God is Love, which God is, and God is the only thing that really exists in reality – whether it is a form-based substance or a thought as energy – then this energy makes up EVERYTHING. Our origin was God. Therefore, everything you can see, think or touch is God. With this in mind, then everything you look upon is God.

*When you can see AND experience ONLY God in
everyone and everything, that is when you will remember
you are God. This is a very frightening statement to many,
but the truth at times can frighten you. The truth can also
stretch you. The truth also does not need your approval to
be the truth.*

*Jesus was the first person to accept the totality of who He
was. Because of this, He was in charge of the unfolding of
the planet Earth. The energy that makes up Jesus has
countless deities and helpers at his disposal. He is
referred to as an elder brother in the Bible, and that is an
excellent metaphor. If He is your brother, then the
inherent equality is set. An elder brother shows you how
to do what He can do. He is also a guide to get you back
home. He loves you with a Love the world cannot
conceive of.*

*Jesus is definitely not asking you to emulate him at the
form level. He is not asking you to carry the old rugged
cross, nor to be crucified, but He does want you to allow
Him to guide you in the awakening process. He knows
who you are as a perfect child of God. And within each
step on your journey, He never deviates from His singular
purpose of guiding you back home. Because He has
achieved what all of us are capable of, He can collapse
time, and thus shorten the awakening process for each of
us. Remember He is but a thought away."*

The Buck Stops Here:

*"I have laughed when I hear someone say 'The buck stops
here.' Isn't that how you think? Actually, that is very
comforting to most on your planet because then you don't
have to think any more about it. You sit back and take
orders, and then you feel this relieves you from taking
responsibility for your actions. So if the situation turns out*

sour, you can always say, 'Well, he/she told me what to do.'

This also serves another purpose. If you are following orders, then you can't feel guilty for your actions because, after all, you are just following orders. It is amazing how that egoic mind of yours diverts guilt outwardly. I am not singling out the military system, but it is a great example of taking 'orders.' You have the lower-level personnel, followed by higher ranking individuals as you 'climb the ladder' to success. And business operations typically mirror the military system. Because of our inability to see the world unlike ourselves, we naturally have to depict a God and hierarchy that mirror how we see people and authoritative systems that are around us.

Our egoic mind then naturally depicts a God at the top of this hierarchical ladder and thus notifies us we must 'climb the ladder' back to God. This climbing varies greatly based on which religion you happen to be focused on and the doctrines it sets forth. Just about every religion and modality has its do's and don'ts, all based on how one should act externally.

Before I go any further, it must be stated that I am not saying any religion or modality is wrong or one is better than another, because if their intention is God, you can still obtain that state of Oneness from your chosen religion or modality. Remember, God will ultimately be at the end of each road or modality you have chosen. Because of the inherent concept of good/bad within most religions and modalities, the rules can be very time consuming and exhort an enormous amount of pain and guilt in the process. It is important to realize that much of this pain is unnecessary.

If God is Love and that is all She is, then what emanates from Love is Love. This energy knows of nothing else; it is completely oblivious to any other emotion. And this is the

*key to understanding God. If God is Love and Love is
energy, then one can say God is energy. And if energy
makes up everything, then God is in everything, and,
therefore, everything is God. Do you not see the logic? If
the first concept is true, the others must follow."*

We Are God:

*"I know some of you will perceive the concept of God as
energy as being rather impersonal, but be thankful that
God is pure Love and Energy. If God is anything other
than Love and Energy, then God would not be God. And
since our true nature is in complete alignment with God,
then who we are is also Love and Energy. We are love
and energy and, as such, we are incapable of
experiencing anything other than an all-encompassing
Love. This Love literally makes up everything – both the
seen and the unseen within our universe.*

*Everything on your planet was first a thought in the Mind
of God. Because of the nature of thought, it must be made
manifest into something you can feel, touch, and taste. As
long as you maintain your attention on the Totality of
Now, what you produce on your side of the veil will bring
you great joy.*

*Even your Bibles point to the collective whole of God. It
reads, 'Ye are gods.' And Jesus stated, 'I and the Father
are one.' He also goes on to tell you that whatever he can
do, you can do too, and even greater things. Well, if Jesus
is one with God, which He is, and we are One with Jesus,
which we are, then we all make up the embodiment of
God.*

*Another way one might want to look at it is to picture all
the cells that make up your body, all trillions of them.
Each group of the cells has a different function, and these*

cells are completely unaware of other cells performing a different function, but collectively they make up the body. Within the body each cell is of equal importance, and each cell knowingly or unknowingly is dependent upon the other cells to perform their function.

We keep giving you different ways to look at the concept of God. The reason is that it takes many ways to present this most powerful concept that has been brought forth. To many, this will bring great joy that is beyond what this world has to offer. But if one cannot accept it, at least bring yourself to the realization that God is Love, and this Love is the only emotion within God. If one can accept that, then one can see why this type of God would never need to forgive you. God's unconditional love is incapable of condemnation. Because God is ONLY Love He is incapable of recognizing sin in anyone, and therefore He has no need for forgiveness.

But if one holds onto the ancient belief that God has chosen a certain group of people to bring forth His messages, then one would have to conceive of a judgmental, vindictive God. Unfortunately, this type of God is portrayed throughout various religious modalities that are prevalent throughout your planet. And with this belief you will eventually dive into a downward tailspin of fear.

Remember, if God is Energy and Love, then God and Energy are one. Again, since your scientists have proven that EVERYTHING is energy, then God is everywhere. Therefore, one can sum it up by saying God is many, but also God is One. The reason for the previous statement is to bring you to the realization that the many is made up of the one. All of you, the many, are one with and in God. God is you. You are God."

Choosing Once Again:

"Your eyes look upon a world that filters back to you the illusion of numerous choices daily. Actually, the egoic world holds no choices. They are all the same in that each choice leads you away from your divine purpose. Each decision, made within the frequency of the egoic mind, will always be wrapped in fear. Therefore, the result will always eventually be fearful.

Oh, the ego will have you on a constant external search through a myriad of obstacles with the hope that another way from fear can be found. Notice how that statement is true within all areas of your life. You are constantly trying to come up with something external to fix an internal problem. That is all the egoic world can hold out for you.

But there is another choice, another alternative once you understand that each choice within the egoic world will eventually lead to despair. Perhaps you feel you must try them all, and that is okay, but in each choice the pain will be felt. In some choices, the thorns are felt immediately. In others, it may take a while before the pain is recognized.

The choice to listen to the Voice for God isn't really a choice once you realize the illusionary nature of the other choices. The choice to listen to the Voice for God is really the choice to listen to your true Self. In accepting who you are, you have become co-creators with God and your only desire becomes, 'How can I in this moment make a choice that will extend the Love of God?' You will have no other desire but to be that One!"

Oneness:

"Oneness is a concept that is difficult to understand because you look at things as being separate. And how

can you not? In the world of dualism there are separate things and people with separate and individual needs and desires. So from an Earthy form-based perspective, Oneness is a spiritual myth. But let's look at what creates the form.

What creates form is thought. Now, if one creates form coming from the egoic mind, one will experience separate things. Then each thing it looks upon will be placed into one of two categories – good or bad. It will not see the connection to love that makes each thing or person it sees as part of the whole. Only when one comes from a place of Love will one see and truly feel the Oneness that blankets everything. It really isn't that difficult if one realizes everything one sees is an aspect of oneself. And if that thought is tied to the Voice for Truth, one cannot help but see the commonality of love in everything.

Being in Oneness is always a matter of choice. This world is a world of contrast – hot and cold, white and black, male and female, right and wrong, etc. If we allow this loving energy to be us, then The Holy Spirit will show us the difference between love and fear. When we finally realize that fear, as an aspect of the egoic mind, truly has nothing to offer us, then fear will no longer have power over us. At this point you will know to associate pain with the ego and peace with the Voice for Truth. With this knowledge in our mind, the desire to be in the state of Love will always over-ride the desire to go back to the old antiquated ways of dealing with egoic issues in our life.

This state of Oneness requires no control, defenses, nor manipulation but instead offers peace. This Oneness is now a body that serves a divine purpose and can now live through divine guidance. Once you are in Oneness you will experience a love that has no parallel on this planet. When you are in this state you will only have one thought, 'How can I serve my brothers and sisters?' There will be no lack or wanting of anything. You cannot lose anything

*because reciprocal interactions are now seen as lacking.
Each decision will be a win/win for both parties. You will
no longer identify with being a body. You will know you
are a soul in a body with a purpose of extending Love and
that Love will permeate your entire being."*

If God Had A Body:

*"If God had a body He would want to let everyone know
they are loved. He would make sure that each of you
understands you have only made mistakes and mistakes
only require a change in thought and behavior. He would
want you to know that you have never left your Source
and we are all one. Also, God would want you to know
that everything you desire is but a thought away. God
would, of course, have to do this differently for each
person. People can only accept so much Love on your side
of the veil. You will see as this chapter unfolds that is
exactly what God is doing every day. God does appear
amongst you in a body in two ways. We will describe them
individually because that is how you experience it, but in
reality they are one in the same.*

*The first way God appears in body is rather rare and
usually only occurs when some type of shift is about to
take place on your planet. This is when God will actually
incarnate in a body to help bring forth certain messages
that could not have been heard in any other manner. Or
God will appear when messages need it to come forth in a
certain setting, for the benefit of a group of people that
have been lagging in the unfoldment process. All these are
rather rare on your planet because of the second way God
appears.*

*The second method of God transforming his Divine
Energy into your planet is through the God part of each of
you. Every time you make the choice to listen to the Voice*

of God, which permeates the planet, you are letting God experience what it feels like to have a body. The body really isn't a hindrance to expressing Love unless you use the body as something other than the purpose given it by God. The purpose ascribed to it by God is simply to allow God to use your body as a vortex through which Love can stream forth.

God needs no body sensations but does need the body to do God's work. By far the vast majority of people on your planet are incapable or unwilling to allow God to use their body for various reasons, unworthiness usually tops the list, but sacrifice usually underlies this enormous fear within each egoic mind on the planet.

When you allow God to be God, then you have reached the highest form of communication. In this state there is actually no difference between your Spirit Self and God. Allowing God to be God also means allowing others to be themselves, allowing events in the world to be as they are without making any demands or judgments upon them. Not having demands is kind of difficult to do when you have an investment with just about everyone and everything in which you interact.

So in wrapping up the question, I am sure this information didn't show up the way most would have expected. Why; because you are looking at God as an individual deity. And, yes, God is singular, but God is also one with everything you see. So, as stated before, God is One, but God is many and the many are the singular One.

This is not difficult to understand when you are God, because God only sees God. God looks at a tree and sees only God. God looks at a mother nursing her child and sees God. God looks at a mother who has just lost her child and sees only God. Be that One!"

You are here to birth
in time what cannot
be contained in time

Chapter 8: The Power of Intention

The Purpose You Give to Whatever You Do:

"Remember, it is the purpose you give something that will determine whether it will bring you joy or pain. In and of itself the body is neutral like everything else on your planet. But your body has a purpose, and there is no exception to that law. PURPOSE is the key to understanding EVERYTHING you bring forth on this planet.

You must give everything the purpose of love, or it will eventually come back to sting you. You will know which purpose you have given something, someone, your body, or other people's bodies, by what messages they bring back to you. If your body is hurting, you have used it wrongly. Sorry, but no exception.

The key word that We will be constantly using throughout this book is the word 'purpose.' Purpose is the key to everything. Give something the purpose of something other than love and that is what it will mirror back to you. It's a very simple law: what you give you receive. Very simply, your intention sets your cause and effect. That is the law, and spiritual laws operate whether you agree, like, dislike, approve, or even believe they do or don't exist. Earthly laws such as gravity operate in a similar fashion and do not need your approval or belief to work. It is important that you understand these spiritual laws so you can use them in a way that will bring your heart joy.

We laugh on this side of the veil as we watch you give the body properties it doesn't really possess. You use words like 'reflects' and even assign it to having certain characteristics, like colds or other bodily ailments. When

*you say something like, 'I have a cold,' it is actually like
describing you as being a cold.*

*Your body can have the appearances of having a cold, but
remember you are not your body. So technically speaking,
you can never have a cold. So the statement, 'I have a
cold,' is a lie and an illusion. Remember, we said earlier
that your body is simply a gauge, and a cold is simply
indicating something to you. Ask your body what it is
trying to tell you, and you will be surprised at what it will
tell you. Become friends with your body; understand it
and it will speak to you.*

*You even speak of bodies as having split or multiple
personalities. I have to laugh when I hear things like this,
as if this is something new. Everyone that has an ego has
at least two personalities. One is their egoic voice, and
the other is the Voice for Truth. Any other personality is
simply your egoic mind coming up with an altered
personality to avoid embracing and transcending some
misaligned thought."*

Your Body as Your Gauge:

*"Your body is an instrument, vehicle, gauge and an
expression of your mind. When we speak of the mind, we
are not referring to the brain. The brain is the gray matter
in your skull that the ego stores information in. Your mind
is actually located outside the body. This fact has been
proven through vast testing done by your scientists. The
testing shows that the energy of your mind is actually
located above your head.*

*When you project a thought from your mind, that thought
produces a certain emotional frequency that the mind
registers and then categorizes into one of two frequencies.
The scientific community labeling will be different than*

the way We will label these two frequencies. One is the egoic aspect of the mind, and the other is that part of your mind that has never been disconnected from its Source. This aspect of your mind is constantly speaking to you, as is the egoic part, but always with drastically different motives.

The egoic part of your mind receives information that supports its belief that you are separate from your Creator and your brothers and sisters as well. This naturally leads to feelings of unworthiness and lack. It also leads to subconscious desires to punish yourself to atone for the guilt you have heaped upon yourself. This guilt lies buried under a cloak of a meaningless persona used to shield. This egoic expression of the false self believes it can 'save' you through the dynamics of projection, but one truly never leaves the treadmill, and the feelings of shame and guilt eventually return to rear their ugly heads.

The egoic mind, ever aware of the Voice for Truth, tries to negate its presence. If that attempt fails, it tells you that you could not possibly be worthy of such a divine purpose because of your past transgressions. The mighty Voice for Truth is constantly aware of whom you are, and its singular purpose is to lead you to the total remembrance of the essences of who you are as a child of God. It tells you that you have never sinned, merely made choices that were not in alignment with Love. Its unwavering knowing of who you are gently guides you in this awakening process. This Voice of God has infinite patience, and with each step taken on this road the need to listen to the egoic voice finally begins to dissolve.

Our bodies, therefore, are merely gauges to indicate to us which voice we have chosen to listen to in that particular moment in time. The body can be experienced within time or in a timeless state. You are in a timeless state while you are listening to the Voice for God. The body's real identity comes from being a vortex for Love. The body becomes a purposeful instrument when it extends the Love of God.

In and of itself the body is neither good nor bad, but simply a gauge that indicates which voice you are presently hearing. You should honor your gauge and thank it for talking to you. That's what gauges do; they indicate to you certain things that you need to be mindful of. I am sure none of you ignore the gauges in your car or your house. You probably monitor your interactions with others and how they might perceive you. That, too, is also a gauge.

How does your body make you feel? Does it bring you joy, or is your body limiting you from doing what you would like to do? Listen to your body. It is constantly talking to you. The body is like looking at your car with all the gauges – temperature, oil, speed, odometer, gas, etc. All of these gauges are telling you something, and when they indicate a certain thing, you take action. You don't get angry at your gas gauge when the needle is pointing to 'E' do you?

Be thankful you know you need to take a certain action. If not taken, it will likely produce a result that will eventually bring you some form of discomfort. Your body is doing the same thing. It is constantly speaking to you and telling you which voice you are listening to. Be grateful for your body; it is a wonderful "instrument" that helps navigate you to the total remembrance of who you are. Be kind to other bodies that walk the path in the awakening process of the Totality of Now. For most, the body will be the best indicator of where you are on your path to your Oneness with the Totality of Now.

There have been those who have been able to maintain a body on your planet for centuries in perfect health. Actually, the word 'health' is a misnomer, as is 'sickness.' Both are merely a by-product of one's thinking. Sickness, like everything else on your planet, serves a purpose. And when that insane purpose is addressed, the need to attach oneself to a sick body vanishes, as a vaporous cloud in the early morning gives way to the sun.

Those that have been able to maintain a physical body for centuries on your planet can clearly see sickness does not serve the purpose of love. Why, because God has given the body the purpose of love and love knows not of sickness. The only true purpose for your body is the extension of love, and when your body simply mirrors these divine thoughts, there is no sickness.

When we identify with the Totality of Now, we stop looking at ourselves as being limited to a physical body, which is tied to the Earthly laws of time and space. While in the Totality of Now you are no longer controlled by the laws of medicine or other laws associated with age or gender. Those laws are true if you identify yourself as a body, but one's identification need not be tied to the body. The body can be a useful instrument that allows the one occupying the body to perform the tasks assigned to it by God.

We are not saying that the laws of medicine are not true, and we are not here to say that you have done something wrong if you need medical assistance. What we are saying is that if you identify yourself as a body, these laws do exist. But you are not a body and sickness is of the mind for which there is no pill, so if you are unable to heal the body with Love then take whatever you feel you need to 'heal' your body. But, remember, there is no pill that will remove the guilt in the mind that caused the bodily ailment. If you have prayed and asked for clearing of all your guilt and the symptom still lingers, then by all means use something that will alleviate the pain.

When your mind has totally accepted this identification with your all-inclusive Oneness, then your body, other bodies, and the world will no longer have the illusion of authority over you. This assumption is based on your total identification with your being spirit and the pure energy of the Love of God. Oh, you do have a body, but it merely is a vehicle to transport you around for two reasons, to be a vortex of love and to complete your purpose for being here. Be kind to your body and love it. Be kind to other bodies and love them. Be kind to Mother Earth and love her."

Limiting Beliefs:

"Limiting beliefs are those thoughts that keep you from hearing the Spirit voice from within you and living the loving life God has intended for you. Differences only exist in your egoic mind, so lay aside those limited beliefs and Be the One who remembers who you are. These messages I am giving you will stretch some of you, but their sole purpose is to help you remember who you are.

You look at the world and your body as being different or disconnected from the God part of you. You, therefore, are on a constant search for this elusive Love, always outside yourself, kind of like a dog chasing its tail. In reality, Love and the God part of you are inseparable, one depends on the other. In your world you understand cause and effect, your most basic law, but you can't have an effect without a cause and vice versa. One creates the other. I, (Anderson) have gone nowhere; I am still here with you. The energy of God that created me is still extending itself. Even your scientists can tell you the universe is constantly expanding."

Do What Brings You Joy:

"Joy is the feeling that engenders an emotion that one wants to share with others. Joy is also a feeling that lays dormant in most that walk your planet. You believe Joy is your reward and can only be experienced at the completion of something, and that is the reason most of you on Earth experience very little joy in your lives. It is like working 'X' amount of hours a week and joy comes in the form of a paycheck, but, for most, the amount of the paycheck they end up receiving leaves little room for joy. This level of thought filters through most minds on the planet and keeps you from having the joy you deserve in every moment of each day.

Do you not see how you have compartmentalized everything on your planet? No wonder it is a daunting task trying to make yourself or someone else happy. Joy, from the egoic mind, is always associated with the getting of something. Thus the repression of one's fears is equated with joy. Therefore, when you don't get what you want, you end up experiencing an emotion other than joy.

Until one comes to the realization that the above definition of joy and pain are the same, then one merely wanders aimlessly seeking joy where it cannot be found. When coming from the egoic mind, you are disconnected from the knowledge that you are responsible for your feelings of both joy and pain. For the egoic mind both feelings are conditional, a heads-or-tails illusionary choice that never brings you joy. Joy can only be experienced when one listens and follows what the Voice for Truth is guiding them to do. Therefore, let your 'doing' be infused with WHO you really are and then everything you do will bring you joy."

When you choose to live
with love rather than fear,
that is when you begin to
give all a Divine Purpose

Chapter 9: Divine Purpose

Choosing to be Here:

"Before we made the choice once again to come to planet Earth, we literally sat with enlightened beings, which you might want to call 'advisors.' This 'counsel' of beings discussed with you the type of journey you would like to undergo in your individual awakening process.

Because of the particular path you have chosen, you will align yourself with certain entities/people to help bring your individual mission into fruition. The process not only includes making the choice of who you will have as parents, mates, and friends, it also determines what parts of your path merges with theirs. The decision for one's parents is probably the most important decision for any given incarnation and typically has the largest impact on your path and the completion of your agreed-upon individual learning and assignments.

This is how things are normally done before one makes the choice to come back in form to planet Earth. Notice the above paragraph uses the word 'individual' because the vast majority of people can only handle their own unfoldment from an individual perspective. There are others – and, once again, rather rare but becoming more prevalent – that choose to take on a role that will help the planet in its awakening. Those who choose such a role know before leaving the other side that their assignments usually involve a great deal of pain. But once they know and recognize their role on your side of the veil, the potential for healing not only themselves but the planet is enormous. Remember, choices made before one incarnates can be adjusted as one walks the journey back to their total remembrance of Now.

Embrace the role of the parent and child relationship and give it a divine purpose. Your parents can be your greatest teacher. At the deepest level you chose them, so ask the Voice for Truth how you can change your relationship with them from one of fear to one of love. Be that One!"

Desires:

"Because your identification is tied to a body, My Beloved Brothers and Sisters, you have desires. It is impossible on your planet not to have them, so desires in and of themselves are not bad, but the purpose you give them is what we are concerned with. The word 'purpose' is the key to your happiness because it will determine what plays out in your life. Purpose is the one word that will determine whether something will eventually bring you joy or pain. If the purpose is anything less than Love, you will feel the thorns of pain at once, or they may come up at a later time. But they will come to the mind that brought them eventually, and that is part of the karmic spiritual laws. It is at the point you ask, "Where did that come from?" that you must remember that at one time or another you put this reaction into your own path. Unfortunately, sometimes you will not be able to connect the pain with the correlating action or thought that produced the discomfort.

The more one becomes connected to their divine purpose, the faster their thoughts are manifested. You will have the thought, and then you will see its manifestation. But because our egoic mind has taught us we are unworthy, we sometimes block our good from coming to us in these variable ways. The reason for not seeing ourselves as the culprit in our demise is our outward projection of our deep-seated fear of feeling unworthy of Love.

There is nothing you can do on your planet that is purely
Divine Love, nor, conversely, is there anything you can do
on this side of the veil that is unloving. Love is your
purpose, your intent, and the 'why' you are doing what
you are doing, and it is what you should be doing. This is
the reason for everything, and there is no exception, and
it will determine what your eyes will show you as a result
of your thoughts. You are the artist of everything you are
presently painting on your screen. The egoic mind is only
concerned that the form is wrapped up in a nice package.
The ego is only interested in appearing 'good' within its
perception of its world, and this perception is usually void
of compassion and love."

Seeing What is Real:

"If you pay attention to your desires and wants, you will
realize the commonality of your desires, which is solely
that of keeping you focused on apparent external needs.
With the focus on your illusionary needs and the hopeful
repression of your fears, you keep yourself at bay from
your one true desire. The only desire that can ever bring
you joy – and should be your singular purpose for being
here – is extending Love from within your most holy mind
and heart out to the world. When your desires are in
alignment with Love, then your fear-based desires will no
longer serve a purpose and will naturally dissipate.

Hopefully, this realization will lead you to give your
desires a Divine purpose. Until then all your interactions
will be habitual, in that you will keep expressing and
projecting actions to support your underlying need to
remove this deep-seated feeling of guilt. Guilt takes on an
almost endless array of forms, but the purpose is always
the same – to project outwardly the deep-seated guilt that
each separate being feels deep within. The more
unworthiness one sees outside, the better one feels. This is

85

*only because your egoic mind tells you that if it is seen
outside, it can no longer be within.*

*Such is this insane concept when one clearly looks at the
dynamics of projection. When one really looks at your
egoic thought systems, denial and projection is all it is
capable of offering you. Within this insane belief, we love
the bad guy. We want the bad guy for numerous reasons,
and we will attract them, with the ultimate reason of
holding them up against your assumed innocence. For if
evil is seen outside, one doesn't have to go inside and will
naturally have to fix the seemingly external bad guy.*

*You see, wherever you put your attention is where you
will perceive the problem. If your perception tells you it is
external to yourself, you will naturally seek to solve the
problem externally. If you realize the insanity of
projection and the way it permeates your planet, you will
have to come to the realization that the dynamics of
projection defies both your Earthly laws as well as
spiritual laws. Projection, as it is defined, is basically the
heaving or throwing outwardly something that lies within
your subconscious mind. Unfortunately, by 'throwing'
those undesirable thoughts outwardly, we only reinforce
them within."*

The Laws of Attraction:

*"The laws of attraction and manifestation overlap in so
many ways. Actually, they are inseparable! Attraction is
like a magnet, as it will draw things to it that line up
within the laws of that specific magnetic field. And this
concept is applicable for what some people would call
good as well as the bad. It matters not whether what you
think is good or bad; it merely follows the law of
attraction.*

86

You cannot circumvent laws because that is what makes them a law. They work under all conditions. Therefore, everything that comes into your life is a result of a thought. That is the law. Most of you react to what your world has given you, and you label these events as either good or bad. Then you proceed to try and minimize the bad and maximize the good. But in this process of external filtering and labeling good and bad, one never figures out how to attract the true good because that only can be achieved by going inward.

Oh, the world does a wonderful job through the mirror principle of showing you what you are thinking. Thus, what you are attracting in your life is exactly what you have sent out into the world. So thank the world for showing you what thoughts you are currently thinking. If you don't like what you see, change your thinking, and the world will mirror back to you the change accordingly. That is the law! Now that you know, put it to work for you.

Remember, we are energy, as is everything else on this planet. And because we have a certain vibrational frequency, that energy attracts things that are beating to the same frequency. On your planet you have a saying that goes 'Like attracts like.' Actually, a better way to define projection would be to say one sees whatever vibration and thoughts they are holding within.

So if you have a dominant thought of unworthiness, that core belief will cover each of your interactions on your planet. This is why people can see the same event and have a completely different view or interpretation of the event and what happened to each person involved. Another person who witnessed the same event will interpret it through their own filter, and it will appear different to them, and each of their world views will prove each of them correct. They can back up what they believe because the world shows them externally a reflection of their inner thoughts.

There are people who will make it financially regardless of the economic uncertainty of the world because they believe they deserve and can attain their goals. Others will struggle regardless of the upswing or downturn in their market place. Think on that awhile!

Because you don't recognize the underlying purpose of your desires and what they mask, you feel each desire holds something of value for you. Notice that the vast majority of your desires are about acquiring things, more money, a mate, house, security, etc. Even the things that you wouldn't necessarily consider external, such as a better education or quitting bad habits, are still all connected to your identification with being a body. You want a better education so the body can have more things. You try to quit the bad habits so the body will feel better. It is very difficult not to be identified with the body on your planet. But you are a spirit. You are pure energy that has accumulated itself into a form you call a body. You must truly realize that this is your truth.

Everything you experience on planet Earth is tied to a timeframe format. Therefore, there is a point A and a point B, and there must be a desire to get to point B. Getting to point B not only takes time, but there must be a desire to get to point B versus point C. Focus your desire on point B, and then truly give point B the purpose of extending Love, and you will finally understand your purpose. So while it is impossible not to have desires on planet Earth, you can and should express each desire wrapped in Love."

Chapter 10: Intervention

Who We are as Energy:

"Energy is the essence that permeates every living thing on your planet. With that definition in mind, inanimate objects also have energy so they are technically alive. Inanimate objects are not alive in the way that we normally speak of, but anything you see on your perceptual viewing screen contains energy and therefore is alive. In reality, energy can manifest itself into any form, but only when its vibrations are lowered to such a point that it can take on a form-based substance.

Our thoughts are energy, and these thoughts, based on their vibration, get projected from either a place of fear or love. When thoughts resonate from a place of love, they extend out love. The body is actually an energy field which paradoxically holds a map of the entire universe. Quantum physics engineers and the scientific community are currently studying how the matrix works and should be able to prove this in the near future.

When your energy is raised to its highest vibrational level, then the neurophysiology within your brain becomes permanently changed. Those who have attained this state truly can be called teachers or healers on your planet. Quantum physics and the scientific community will eventually prove this to be true. Once again, there is going to have to be those in that field who believe that is a possibility before that can occur. We will make sure that is brought into manifestation.

Unless you understand energy and the paradigm shifts that must take place on your planet, these shifts will produce an enormous amount of fear for you. We must clarify the previous sentence. Understanding what energy is and how it operates on your planet is an imperative, but this knowledge does not heal the problem with fear. Healing takes place through a change from within the mind. But for most on your planet there must be a reason to change, and it is our hope to be able to provide you with the reason. Understanding the use of energy will actually solve little unless you take what you have learned here and implement this knowledge into your daily life.

Because your complete identification is wrapped up as being in a body, you may be unable to recognize how energy permeates every aspect of your reality. Your scientists have proved everything is energy. It is a simple matter of what frequency the energy is vibrating. The frequency at which the energy is vibrating determines how or if the being's form takes a physical shape or remains invisible to the naked eye or comes forth as a thought. That is why when a being's form changes or is laid to rest (just a nicer way of saying someone has died), the energy that created that form continues to live on.

Why are you still convinced that what you body's eyes perceive is real? It can only be because you have identified yourself as a body, and because of this identification you have become a reactor to what you view. Your interpretation of what you perceive outwardly seems to determine what emotion you experience within. The emotional energy behind your thoughts will project itself outwardly, and it is this inward belief projected out that will overlay everything in your world. It will ultimately attach itself to whatever you see on this planet. You also believe that what you hear and smell is real. You also believe in what those in power tell you is real and you question not. Until you have the desire to change from within, you will allow the world to dictate how you should feel. This is how you victimize yourselves.

Everything has as its core a certain vibration, and this vibrational frequency extends forth from this dense matter we give reality. This energy is also affected by the one perceiving or observing the object in question. That is why the observer actually can affect what one observes.

The laws that are set forth in your educational and legal books at all levels are hard to disprove because to the believer the world system shows them what they believe. This is the reason why new paradigm shifts are usually experienced on your planet with a great deal of pain, but it is through this pain that some are motivated to take a stance that the world will view as 'radical.' True insightful breakthroughs occur when one has the ability to see change as an opportunity for growth and push through the barriers that were previously held in place.

Therefore, we should express everything with Honor, Compassion, and Excitement. Energy from a Spiritual perspective encompasses the word 'Love' and yet it is formless. For love is unlimited and ever expanding and never dissipates. So who you are at the core of your being is pure energy, pure Love. This essence of who you are is never altered in any manner. When one has an emotion other than Love, then they are in discord with themselves. The true Self never deviates from its Source, which is God. You are pure Love which is in perfect alignment with your true Self. This loving energy that makes up your true essence is constantly expanding and seeking something or someone to attach Itself.

The reason why most people who have incorporated into a body are unable to make contact with those on the other side of the veil is they have identified themselves as a body. You have a body, but you are not your body. You are a mind that is attached to God, and when you truly listen to that part of your mind, you can make contact with anyone who ever walked this planet at any time or within any dimension. The duration of time of passing from this planet has nothing to do with the essence of who they are. They are timeless and always available, just as Jesus laid his body down over 2,000 years ago and is still available to you."

The Need of Intervention:

"Most great leaders while they walked this planet were at some time considered radical. Be honest, think of those that impacted and changed the world. All were considered radical but wavered not in the messages they presented. Look at some of your great spiritual leaders; they were not welcomed with their new ideas while they walked this planet. At the time these truths were brought forth they were very unsettling to the established system. This was the reason they were labeled as 'provoking radical views to the masses' and considered radicals. In fact most had to lay their bodies down to truly get their messages across. Actually, that is part of the Divine Plan, to bring forth these rather radical points of view to a planet that doesn't accept them when they are first brought forth. Then these great leaders leave their body for numerous reasons, but primarily so that people could focus on the messages and not the messenger.

Whenever the messenger delivering the messages is still in a bodily form, then people will question them about the messages or look for the messenger to help them. Again, most people would want to idolize the messenger and not the messages they bring forth. The reason for the idolizing perception within the masses is their unknown unwillingness to implement the messages. As I mentioned in <u>Anderson Speaks</u>, the ultimate reason for me laying my body down was that no one would have taken these messages seriously coming from a 22-year old.

Think of all of those you have idolized in politics, sports, military or even certain friends and family members who have made a difference for you. Their controversial messages do bring attention to them, and because they are now being focused on, they are also going to be scrutinized. This is actually part of the plan also because if these messages are looked at with an open mind, one will have to see the validity in each statement. We would want them to be put under a microscope.

As we will state in other places of this book, very seldom do we intervene on this side of the veil. We are circumventing the normal process at this time in history because of the shifts that will be taking place. These shifts will be taking place in a short period of time, which makes our current messages of uttermost importance at this time.

We must circumvent the normal method of the unfolding process, and We will do that by placing certain people in a position to prove these messages. Energy and purpose are the two main concepts that one will have to grasp to understand these spiritual laws being brought forth. Be kind to yourself, allow the energy of love to open itself up to you, and you will be in a position to adjust to any shift that will take place on your planet.

You – yes, We are speaking to YOU – must be able to align your thoughts to higher vibrational frequencies so that when the shifts do occur you will be able to help those that might perceive these shifts as the end of the world or as God's punishment. Of course, none of this is true. These shifts are simply a way of waking up the planet so it can align with the Voice for Truth. This will be discussed in greater detail in the chapter on planetary shifts.

Your brothers and sisters on this planet need to see things as being a process, so it appears to you that way, but only because you cannot see the immediacy of NOW. So it will appear, for the most part, that as individuals we have to incarnate numerous times to attain this level of awareness. The sheer number of these enlightened beings is of the uppermost importance because of the shifts that will be taking place. Because of that, the number of Ascended Masters who will be taking a physical body for the first time will increase drastically.

Actually, enlightened beings are even more prevalent on your planet than ever before. Because of the impending events that will be taking place on your planet, the normal evolution process will be circumvented. We will be placing Ascended Masters on your planet to help with the events that will be shortly unfolding on your planet.

The Ascended Masters will have the ability to be in numerous places at the same time, known in some modalities as bi-location. While Jesus walked this planet He was in numerous places all over the world at the same time. That is why there were similar accounts of someone teaching followers to remember the Totality of Now. Each of these persons gave basically the same message. In reality, the messages all came from the same person or, better put, from the energy of the same person.

You will know who the Ascended Masters are when you are ready to start your path. Until then, you'll wander aimlessly wondering why God has deserted you. If you are one of those who are unable to remember your path while you are here, then you will become numb to others and yourself and spend the remainder of your life doing senseless things, and then you will lay the body down. Please realize that these enlightened beings will manifest in your life in whatever form is most suitable for you. If you need them in a physical body, they will appear that way for you. If you need a message through words, that is how you will hear them. If either of those methods would potentially produce any fear in your most holy mind, then you might just receive your guidance through this book.

It matters not how one receives guidance. One method is no better than another, because one person can hear a voice or another connects through dreams. What is of uttermost importance is that you ask for guidance, and you are open to receiving it! When you are truly ready, the form most acceptable to you will bring forth the messages that will inspire you.

You will be given the energy to carry out your part in the overall plan. You will no longer be concerned with others' opinions of yourself. Why; because you will have become a vortex for Love to flow through you and, in reality, now you have become an Enlightened One. You will smile more. You will recognize and be recognized by others on the same path, whether they express their purpose in the form you have chosen or whether they have chosen another.

Others will think you are just the same. They will still judge you from the past and not see who you have become. Why; because they are stuck in the past and believe the past makes up the core nature of their existence. They cannot see things in the Now because of their fear of Love. But even in their egoic insanity they are smart enough to choose you to interact with so that they may project their repressed fears onto you. Because of this they are deserving only of your love. They are simply crying out for help and love, and with this knowledge in your heart, your only response can be love. If you offer anything less you are saying their thoughts about the past are true, and you have forgotten who you are. Be that One!"

Ascended Masters:

"Within the context of this book, Ascended Masters can be described as someone that has risen above the egoic race and sexism consciousness of the prevailing norm of the planet. Every one of you at your core Spiritual Self is an Ascended Master, though very few recognize who they are. Those that have risen above the egoic race and sexism consciousness have dropped the need to hold onto their egos and can now project love onto all that they come into contact.

The normal way of ascending to this state is the gradual removing of your undesirable egoic mind. This process would have been considered somewhat on the cutting edge, which is true given the slow evolution that has been the norm on your planet. But because of the upcoming shifts, the slow evolution will have to be circumvented. Each step, each offering in the forgiveness process will now be heavily supported by those that have already become Ascended Masters, whether they are presently in a bodily form or on the other side of the veil.

What might have taken several lifetimes, can now be done in the matter of months. Dedicate yourself to your purpose, listen with your heart, stop playing small to fit in, and the world of peace and joy will open before your eyes and reveal a new world unfolding before you. When you reach this state, you will now have become part of the Atonement, and you will help those that are walking blindly as you once did.

There are many who have walked this path in previous centuries, but never so many at one time. They have done so through many paths of self-evaluation and learning. There are so many more opportunities for learning now than there has ever been before. Search and you will find. Be the one who accepts this path and is open to learning all that is available to you."

Accelerating Enlightenment:

"This planet has never had a more dire need of enlightened beings than at this time. Because of the impending energy shifts that are currently taking place, the raising of the collective consciousness of the planet is imperative. As stated before, the energy coming into the planet is all good loving energy, but be that as it may, it will engender fear for those who are not in close vibrational proximity.

Therefore, a plan has been undertaken to assist as many as possible to reach a state of accelerated enlightenment. There has been a number of enlightened being placed on your planet to help with the upcoming shifts. This process will circumvent the normal process because of the events that will be taking place on your planet. Typically the normal process of removing the egoic aspect of your minds for most takes many incarnations. The planet no longer has the luxury of time.

Because of the urgency, We will place certain enlightened beings on the planet that have by-passed the need to have a body to work out their ego. These enlightened beings, for the most part, will be what you would call very ordinary people. But they will influence others to do great things. Once again, for the most part, many will stay in the background, but those who are ready to embrace ushering in a new world will know and embrace their messages.

With the increase in energy coming into the planet, everyone now has access to an accelerated plan presently unfolding on your planet. The normal way of removing guilt that would usually take lifetimes can now be accomplished in a relativity short period of time. Once again, this process is open to all because the increased energy is available to all. Each act of forgiveness will literally lift the giver and receiver out of time, and place them closer and closer to the ultimate learning that there is nothing but God.

Of course, there are certain modalities that will help one in their individual process of awakening such as: meditation, sound/music, forgiveness, releasing the undesired thoughts implanted in your cellular memory, and many more. But none will work unless one is ready. If one is ready, then the Voice for Truth will guide that individual by whatever modality is best suited for the individual in the quickening process of enlightenment."

Chapter 11: The Power of Love and Compassion

Love:

"'Love' is a word defined in many different ways on your planet. What an all-inspiring beautiful word, but probably one of the most misunderstood and misquoted words in any language. Because of the various meanings – and We will show them to you – We are going to put the word 'love' in reference to the first two definitions with a lower case 'l' as you will see. Then at the end we will put the word 'Love' with a capital letter to signify what true Love really means.

You use love to describe how you may feel about many subjects other than the romantic and parent/child relationship. Things or topics you might love include, but are not limited to: money, work, sports, nature, etc. The word love is also associated with the repression of one's fears. Because Love is the opposite of fear we believe that love will suppress our fears. These fears include the feeling of being alone and the fear of not having what one believes one should have.

All fear stems from your repressed association with the loss of love. These fears are brought forth from your subconscious mind and can wreak havoc in your life. This is just a nice way of saying, 'There is something or someone on my viewing screen who has done something to cause me to lose my peace.' Your ego will then seek out ways to rearrange what actually occurred and project it outward in such a way that when you again view the person or event, it will bring you whatever peace you are desperately seeking. You give the completion of that process the word 'love.'

Once again, this is applicable whether we are referring to a romantic partner, platonic relationship, or inanimate objects. That's why you have the saying 'Love is Blind.' You become blind as your ego chooses to interpret the other person's actions in a way that best suits the outcome you desire.

Be honest, when you desire something and then you get it, you feel better, and there is nothing wrong with that. Just please don't call that love. Or when someone says something bad about you because they don't like you, and then suddenly they decide that they do like you after all, this makes you feel better. Or when they say good things about you, you feel better. And there is nothing wrong with that, just don't call that love. When your body is causing you pain, and you take something to remove the pain, and it makes you feel better, that also is great, just don't call it love.

Your ego calls that love and it has you on a constant search for love externally for the singular purpose of pushing those repressed fears back into the subconscious mind. Thus this searching outwardly and accumulating is associated with the emotion of love. Once again, this is applicable regardless for all those seeking love outwardly."

The Ego and Love:

"One of reasons for this book is to help you realize the insane premises on which the egoic thought system presents itself to my brothers/sisters, and the gross mental misalignment that is the result of listening to this false self. Hopefully, when you see its insanity you will make

*the only other true alternative choice you have before
you. If you truly see what your egoic thoughts have to
offer, you would run the other way in stark terror and
never look back. But in the egoic state of mind in which
most of you have been indoctrinated, you never really see
what truly is being offered. The only thing the ego can
offer you is the denial of your true Self and this is the core
reason for all your seemingly external problems.*

*Those who identify with this false egoic-self do not know
who they really are, nor do they recognize the gift behind
the fear. How could one possibly see their brothers and
sisters as their ticket back to God when viewing it from a
thought system that is diametrically opposed to such a
concept? After all, it is your brothers and sisters you
believe who have robbed you of your joy. It always boils
down to this in the egoic mind. 'I was peaceful until this
happened to me,' or 'this didn't happen.' Or, 'I was
peaceful until this person did this' or 'this person didn't
do what I deemed worthy for them to bestow upon me.'*

*We are bringing forth these messages with as much
playfulness and gentleness as possible, but these
messages still have to come forth. So no matter how they
are presented, they are apt to bring repressed fears deep
within your subconscious mind to the forefront. Because
of the enormity of that original fear, you have made a vow
with the ego never to look that deep, so you never have
the thought that you could possibly be the common
denominator in all your illusionary fears. Be kind to
yourself. The help you need lies not in the illusionary
offerings of the egoic mind, but in the inner true self and
can only truly come from a place of love and peace.*

*The single decision in your problem-solving egoic arsenal
is that fear has more to offer you than love. It is really the
only problem you have ever had. The enormity of that
original decision is constantly played out on your planet,
over and over. You seem to be constantly making the*

wrong decisions, but they all can be traced back to that original decision to choose fear over love. This original error of choosing fear over love engenders feelings of unworthiness in all areas of your lives. These feelings hide the underlying feeling of 'I am unworthy of God's Love.' To eradicate these feelings you have a deep-seated need to punish yourselves in the mistaken belief that it will atone for your transgressions.

Because of these constant decisions of fear over love, you have created a world that is devoid of Love. Love now has to be sought after and involves a transaction where something has to be given in order to attain this elusive love that is inherently yours. And now this is where reciprocal relationships come into play, not just in the romantic or parent/child relationship, but in each interaction. Other bodies, things or events are now capable of withholding love, and you must give them something to justify the love they could provide you. All this is an illusion, and all illusions are simply something that appears to be real but isn't, and this illusion is no exception.

As the egoic thought system is logical, so too is the mighty Voice for Truth. But its logic is based on truths, and the egoic mind on the illusions of truth. The Voice for Truth tells you quietly and often that you have never separated from God and you have never sinned but simply made mistakes. These mistakes call for correction, not punishment to atone for your errors. It also states that the world is merely a mirror of your thoughts, and your feelings are the result of how you view your world.

If you see a world that produces emotions other than love, you have simply listened to the wrong voice and all you need do is ask the Voice for Truth to give you another way of looking at the events that are transpiring on your screen. This Voice constantly tells you, in the frequency of Love, that you really have only one emotion and that is

Love. Along with that love is a deep desire to join with and help others in their awakening process. To do this you must join with others from a spiritual perspective. This awakening process is easily accomplished when one sees others as either expressing love or crying out for love.

In order to have the love you are so desperately searching for, you must first seek to receive the love that is awaiting you from your Spirit Self. It is there always, bountiful and inextinguishable. You need only be aware to recognize it and own it as your inheritance. Once you have accomplished that, then you will be unable to restrain yourself from helping others to attain the same loving Oneness.

When you are in the energy of Love, and remember that all Love is energy, you cannot but feel that singular emotion. When that feeling fills every core of our being, you can only love yourself and others. Therefore, all of our brothers and sisters are innocent. Why; because you have remembered who you are as this glorious child of God, and with this knowledge you understand they are a glorious child of God as well and therefore as guiltless as you. Be that One!"

Conditional Love:

"Love is such a beautiful word on your planet. But also the one that has caused the most destruction. It is that powerful because of the ambivalent feelings in the offerings of the egoic love. What passes for love for most really isn't really love. Instead it is but an exchange that takes place between two people for the singular purpose of trying to get from the other what each is lacking. If you can acquire from the other what you desire, you love them for their capacity to provide the object you believe will

assist you in the repression of your fears. Such a sorry substitute for love, please choose again.

When the search for love is external and originates from the fear-based part of your mind, then one can never realize true love. The real egoic fear believes that if you don't get what you want, you will eventually look inside and ask the question; 'Why?' Instead, the egoic mind deflects the inward search and begins the process of projection. 'If only that person would change.' 'If only this event would work out the way I planned, I would be happy.' And all too often you listen to this voice. Why; because after all you are on this search for 'love.' And then you add justification to the other thoughts, 'Besides, that person really did do those mean things to me.'

You love to search and seek to find things. It is engraved in your egoic mind, because as long as you are searching for love you feel, 'I must be a good person.' A better word to describe this love is ambivalent love which simply means you really are experiencing two emotions, at least you think that is the case, but actually they are one and the same. The two emotions we are referring to are love and hate.

Most love that is expressed on planet Earth is conditional love. Be honest, watch your emotions. You love someone if. . . (You fill in the blank.) And if they failed to do (You fill in the blank.) you no longer love them. Just that simple fact should indicate to you that the original feeling wasn't love to begin with but actually conditional love. Conditional love is NOT love. Now you can see why it is such a difficult subject to grasp on your planet. The whole world as you know it depends upon conditional love. It is what keeps things 'orderly.' We laugh on this side of the veil at that word 'orderly' because it is just a nice way to control the masses. And everyone runs around feeling that they are in love. Once you have experienced true Love,

*then conditional love will no longer have a place in your
life."*

Unconditional Love:

*"Words are inadequate to describe the unconditional
Love that We have for you, as there is no parallel nor
counterpart to compare it with on your planet. It is this
unconditional Love that you must embrace and carry
forward to all who dwell on your planet. Use this type of
Love to replace all other emotions, and you will be in the
correct mind frame for the coming events. Send your
limitless love out to your families, friends, neighbors, and
all those in your city, state, country and world on a daily
basis and you will be on the right road to making the
world a better place. Visualize surrounding everyone in
God's radiant love, joy, happiness, and the light of truth.
Be that one!"*

Soul Mates:

*"'Soul Mate' is a word that would signify some type of
spiritual completion. It is also a word that might bring
forth feelings of completeness, joy, or a coming together
for a divine connection. And We would have to agree, but
We are going to add one more element for you to attach
to the term 'soul mates.'*

*Webster defines soul mate as, 'A person who is perfectly
suited to another in temperament.' A nice worldly answer,
but one must ask the question, 'Temperament in what?'
The temperament we would insert is your Purpose for
being here on planet Earth. That divine search that
everyone seems to cry out, 'What is my purpose?' or
'Why did I choose to come to the planet at this time?' And*

*this for most people is associated with finding that one
person to help them with their search.*

*The above definition to soul mate would be expanded
upon to mean anyone who helps you to remember who
you are as a child of God. Even the person that brings up
your issues is your soul mate because they are giving you
the opportunity to remove those undesirable thoughts, and
that will bring you closer to the total remembrance of who
you are as a child of God. Notice the title selected for this
chapter, Soul Mates, not Soul Mate. That was done
intentionally, because everyone is your soul mate.*

*We know in this world most are looking for that one.
Looking for just that one can handicap you in many ways.
You will not see the gift others are offering if you are
looking for just the right one. In the search for your
singular soul mate, you will put your life on hold and
eventually feel like a failure or even begin to believe that
God is punishing you for. . . Well, you fill in the blank.*

*On a rare occurrence there are certain people and, for
some, a singular person who is your identical twin
spiritually, who has come here with you on the same
mission, to the same planet, at the same time. IF that
happens for you, so be it, but it is not a realistic goal for
many as it is such a rare occasion. That usually only
happens when We need two people to work together for a
major shift that will take place on this planet. One must
let the belief of a singular person that was specifically
made for you vanish from your mind. In this futile search
you actually hamper yourself and others who have been
placed here to assist you while you are on your journey
back to God. The reason it has the potential to hamper
others is they too are offering you a gift, and by your
refusal to accept it, you can also block their path on their
journey.*

We would strongly suggest that you give everyone equal credibility in their capacity to help you remember who you are as a child of God. When you give all your brothers and sisters that divine purpose, you lay the need down to find that special someone. This will relieve the guilt that is usually associated with the failure to find a singular soul mate. It will also remove a lot of the blame that we project along the journey back to God. With this new search in your awareness you will also remove many excuses you have for failure in various areas of your life.

The second way of looking at love, and given where most of you are on the ladder back to God, this is a very healthy type of love. And this type of love will eventually lead you to the real Love. This process requires you to see the person you are interacting with as your brother or sister who is walking back to God, and their single purpose is to help you to remember who you are. This is not always easy when they are pushing your buttons.

But we will once again come back to the word 'purpose.' What purpose are you giving your brothers and sisters? This purpose will either mirror fear, which is really conditional love or love. I notice Gene feels most people don't see fear and conditional love as the same emotion, but notice in conditional love you constantly have to do something to keep that person's love for you. The fear comes in because you know sooner or later you will do something that does not meet their view of what you should be doing to make them happy, and, as such, you will lose your peace. And that feeling brings you back to fear, no matter how you wrap the gift.

By giving your interactions a divine purpose, which includes remembering who you are and helping your brothers and sisters remember who they are; you become a vortex for Love. Give your interactions the highest Love possible on this planet, a holy Love, a non-conditional Love. This love is not conditional because it recognizes

*that the person you are interacting with is either
expressing love or crying out for help. If they are crying
out for help, which is another way of saying they are
attacking you, you can answer with Love. This Love
always starts with a sincere internal question of 'What is
the most loving thing I can do in this situation?' To the
degree you can sincerely ask such a question will be the
degree the world will mirror back to you the love you
offered.*

*The ultimate way to interact with Love that one day will
permeate your planet is to BE the Love that is emitted
from your true Self. This type of Love is always full,
cannot be depleted, and is always giving. This giving is Its
true nature and distinguishes Itself from the other two
types of love for the reasons just stated.*

*Love was never established to be acquired from another.
For in the attempt to take Love from another you lose
what you seek outwardly. Love, and we speak here of true
Love, comes from within. There is nothing you need do to
acquire this Love; it comes with you because it is you.
With this knowing there is only one thing that you will
want to do and that is to give it away. This feeling of
giving Love away is indescribable once you experience it.*

*This act of giving can only reinforce the Love that allows
the body to heal itself and to extend forgiveness in a place
in dire need of Love. Notice when you are truly connected
to your Source, which is just another way of saying you
realize the Oneness with the Totality of Now, you want
only one thing, and that is to give this Love to others.
When you are experiencing an emotion of love emanating
from your egoic mind, it is always conditional. You know
the difference, and the love bestowed upon another is
always conditional.*

*The contrast of the various types of love on your planet is
good in that it allows you to see how one type of love will*

eventually lead you to feel some emotion that is less then Love. The choice to choose Love will always lead to more feelings of Love, not only for oneself but for all those that one interacts with. Be That One!"

Divine Love:

"Divine Love is the essence that makes one alive, joyful, and exhilarated. And when we speak of Divine Love, we truly mean that if you were devoid of this Love you would cease to exist. There would be no record of you ever having existed on your planet. So who you are at your core being is Divine Love.

That is why you are one with everyone and everything. This Divine Love is continually recreating Love on your planet. Remember, every thought you have produces something. Therefore you are capable of constantly creating Divine Love. Each person has the ability and responsibility to take in everything they look upon with Love in their heart. And with that precious look of Love, a mirroring of Divine Love comes back to the sender, and, thus, it continues in a constant circle of giving and receiving Love.

We ask you now to become that One who accepts your part in God's plan for ushering in a new world. When you accept your part, you have now become part of the Atonement. And the Atonement is just what it states: At-One-Ment – that which is one with God, everyone and everything."

Purpose and Love:

"As long as you have a body, you must give the body a divine purpose. With this divine purpose, you will automatically extend and spread this Love to others who have temporality forgotten who they are. In this coming together process the body will be a useful instrument. This is what we mean when we tell you to give the body the ultimate purpose of extending love.

This doesn't mean one must give up anything they enjoy. All spirit is asking is simply give whatever you are presently doing a divine purpose, and in your intention lies your true lasting joy. Go forth and do what makes your heart sing. Just give it the purpose of extending love. Remember, sacrifice solves nothing but momentarily repressing your fears. We ask you to delete the mistaken belief that sacrifice can and will bring you the love you seek.

Look at what brings you joy, true joy, not the egoic joy of repressing your fears, and allow this love in your heart. When this is accomplished, you will automatically transcend the egoic fear attached to these interactions. When your mission/assignment is complete you will gently lay your body down, with much joy, I might add. Why; because you will no longer have to endure the issues associated with maintaining a body."

Chapter 12: The Paradigm Shifts

Sickness:

"To speak of sickness I will have to speak of the body and energy side-by-side. I say that because you associate sickness as being with the body. Actually, the body is never really sick, nor is it ever really well. Your body is merely a beautiful indicator of your thoughts, a receiving device for indicating what types of thoughts are taking place within your mind. As your gauges in your car indicate the status to which they are connected, so the body indicates the particular thought system to which it has been connected.

The mind that has a thought that is not in alignment with its Source will produce a restriction of energy. This restriction will have to show up somewhere in your world. One way this misaligned thought can manifest itself is through sickness and all the vast array of forms that sickness can attach itself to within your body. Remember all non-alignment thoughts will produce some form of discomfort within the body's sensory feeling nature. Sickness is the way the body gives us feedback as to which voice we are listening to.

These misaligned thoughts block the flow of energy from the mind to the body, and, thus, can take on some bodily form of pain. Once again, this is not the only place these misaligned thoughts project themselves. This restricted flow can take the form of dysfunctional relationships or lack of having enough money to bring your heart joy. But for the purpose of this discussion, we will view the restriction as solely manifesting itself in the form of a bodily condition you refer to as sickness. You should actually thank your body for telling you something is misaligned so that it can respond accordingly.

As with most topics being brought forth in the format of this particular book, the focus will always be on the word 'purpose.' To give something a purpose, it must affect you in some way. That might seem like a perplexing statement, but if something doesn't affect you personally, you give it no attention. Let us suppose there was a mining strike in China, most people in the United States would take very little notice. But suppose you had a stock with its earnings directly affected by that particular mining company, now the strike has your attention.

There is no exception to these spiritual laws that I am presenting in a basic and easily understandable way. Throwing a bunch of statistical information or using impressive words won't motivate anyone to change. But showing them what they think and how these thoughts affect them directly, should cause them to look at the way they think. The goal here is to affect your future interactions with others and allow them to come from a totally different perspective.

It is my desire for you to change your perspective and be motivated through love and not guilt. Guilt will definitely motivate you to do something, but what it will motivate you to do will never produce a good result, and there is no exception to this law either. The best one can hope for is a temporary suspension of one's deep-seated fears that lay dormant in one's subconscious mind. Sooner or later the sting from taking an action based on a guilty thought will have to manifest itself in your world.

I would strongly suggest you start connecting the dots between fearful or guilty thoughts and what they are producing for you. The vast majority of people never make that connection because they have become a puppet to the effects of what they see. Notice I said, 'The effects

*of what they see.' They think they are the effect. You have
to realize you are the CAUSE. Right now, get out a pen
and notepad; the notepad should be the size that you can
keep with you at all times.*

*When something happens, notice your thoughts centered
on an event. (Please do this with something where the
ramifications will be **minor**.) Notice any feelings of guilt
or anger associated with what you are presently
experiencing. Now run with that fearful emotion and let it
play out. Feel it and do what it is directing you to do.
Hate that person, see yourself getting even with them,
and/or see something bad happening to them.*

*Afterwards take notice of how you feel, but don't go
through the forgiving process just yet. Watch how it plays
out. When the finality has come to fruition as a result of
the choices you made, notice them and then ask yourself,
'did it bring you joy?' Also notice that your choices did
not bring joy to any of the other parties connected to your
actions stemming from your fearful egoic mind either.
Take a moment and write down the event, your choice to
choose fear instead of love and the result it produced.*

*Then do this with at least three more events in your life,
and see how each one has produced less than desirable
results. Once again, I would strongly suggest that you do
this with very minor events that have very small
consequences. Now you can start connecting the dots.
This might seem like we are asking you to form a case
study of yourself, and you would be correct.*

*Once you have completed this self-study, your life will
never be the same. You may still make the choice for fear,
but at least now you will not do it subconsciously. You
now have the awareness, you have a choice in which
emotions you will manifest into each interaction you have
and the associated outcome that will result. Going*

forward if you choose to hang onto the emotion of fear, at least you know how it will unfold.

Put yourself in charge by consciously making the choice, even if it produces an undesirable result. The message we are trying to get across is that you are always in charge of your life whether you are consciously aware of it or not. Remember that the mind needs a reason to do something differently. You have just given your mind that reason. This is a simple exercise, but a very powerful one. The mind needs that logical reason to make the choice for love. You have just given the mind the impetus it needs to bring you the healthy choices you so desperately desire.

With this newfound knowledge, hopefully one can see the emotional body is simply a gauge that indicates which thoughts you are tuned in to. You have gauges around you practically all the time. Your car has gauges, and your house is full of gauges. Even when you are out in nature, there are gauges such as the wind and temperature. These gauges are there to solicit a certain response. Once you are aware of these gauges, you may choose to follow the proper response these indicators require or simply ignore them. If your gas gauge indicates empty or the temperature is in your house is very low or it is raining, you should take action. In some sense, everything on your planet is a gauge and demands you take some form of action, and no action is a result of deciding to take no action. Therefore, it is still a decision of taking no action.

Your body is always acting as a gauge, and you have to listen to what it is trying to tell you. If your body appears to be causing you a restriction in movement, then it is trying to tell you that you have made a choice that produced the restriction in movement you are presently experiencing. Until you answer the call to find out what is wrong, the body will keep producing either that particular form of restriction or another form of sickness. It simply is trying to tell you something, and until you listen, it will

114

keep trying to get your attention. Why; because that is its function.

Picture yourself having a friend and you must deliver a certain message to your friend; if you didn't, there would be dire consequences. I truly believe if you called and they didn't answer the phone, you would call again and again, or you would take physical action to see if you could find him/her. Well, that is your body. It simply is trying to tell you something, and until you listen, it will keep trying to get your attention. Why; because that is its function. It is a GAUGE, and that is what gauges do. You can ignore the gas gauge for a while in your car, but eventually it will get your full attention by having the car become immobile.

The body has a singular purpose and will never deviate from what it is designed to do. Therefore, you should thank your body for telling you, through a bodily restriction, that you are playing an old repetitive song that keeps you stuck in the same old, unproductive mode of thinking. Remember, you have connected the dots between unloving thoughts and their results, so be grateful for the beautiful gauge you have at your disposal.

Honor your body. No matter what we do to it, what we feed it, how we treat it, it always tries to heal itself. The ultimate purpose for the body is the extension of Love, and to do that one needs a body that is mobile and able to deliver the messages it is receiving from the Voice for Truth. If you have truly given the body the purpose of extending love, you will need little approval from the world as to how the body should look. This does not mean that we ignore the body or not feed it properly, bathe, or groom. All this needs to be done, but for a different reason. If your body gives you little trouble, you DON'T have to focus so much time on it.

*You might want to get still, breathe deeply, center
yourself and ask your body, 'What are you trying to tell
me?' This will take some practice, but the more you do
this the easier it will be to hear and decipher what it is
trying to tell you. Remember, until you pick up the phone
it will keep ringing.*

*Not only is your body is a gauge, but so is everything else
on the planet, whether it is a living thing or inanimate
object. If you take notice you will see that everything on
Earth is trying to tell you when you are or are not
listening to the Voice for Truth. Therefore, if you are
unable to decode what your body is trying to tell you, get
still so you can ask the Voice for Truth, 'Shoulder, what
are you trying to tell me?' The degree of sincerity of the
question will determine the response you receive. Be kind
to yourself. We know this is new to you. All we ask is a
willingness to be led in the direction of truth. Be that
one!"*

Healing Energy:

*"The energy that is coming into the planet is what
sustains you. As we have mentioned numerous times the
energy coming into the planet is of a frequency never seen
before and will not dissipate but will increase to its peak
between late 2014 or early 2015. If you are in the proper
alignment accomplished by accepting who you are as a
child of God, this energy will bring you more joy than
your heart and mind can possibly conceive of at the
present time.*

*This energy heals everything that is in alignment with its
divine source. It constantly goes forth. It cannot dissipate
or get used up. To many this is such a foreign concept,
because love has no limits. It only knows of love and has
no opposite to compare itself with. It loves you whether*

116

you are aware of its presence, oblivious, or a nonbeliever. For most the final acceptance of this divine energy will occur only when the pain becomes too intense to bear. It is Our desire to help you learn through love and thus dissipate the need to learn through fear. We want you to be a happy learner. But learn you must. You will no longer be able to have the luxury of saying, 'I don't know if I want to do this.' This energy coming in will cause you to do something, either you will be fearful of it or lovingly accept it. We are giving you the tools to allow you to usher this energy in coming from love and therefore realize the benefits of that Love.

This energy heals all forms of self-imposed distractions that you have placed on your viewing screen. And we do mean self-imposed, as it is never – and we mean never – God who is punishing you or causing pain in your life in order to guide you to take a certain action. God is Love and is oblivious to any other emotion. Oh, you may have forgotten who you are at times, but the Voice for Truth will always provide you with a constant reminder to lead you gently back on a journey to your true Self."

The Frequency of Love:

"You are accustomed to using frequencies all the time throughout your day. Your radio has two frequencies, AM and FM and numerous channels that can be dialed up on either frequency. Within the frequency of the egoic mind, the dial knows not of love. Oh, it dresses up the fear to be pretty, for those willing to be deceived. The wrapping does seem to hold something of beauty for those individuals. But those willing to stop playing this sick game of hide and seek with God will clearly see what's behind the wrapping. Therefore, when one is coming from love, one will see the wrapping offers nothing of value.

The frequency of Love is so gentle; it can guide you through a win/win situation with each decision that you are confronted with throughout your day. It never deviates from its appointed path. It never punishes you to teach you a lesson and knows not of sin. This love heals all pain, all past regrets or future fears. Love has no opposite because it is all inclusive. It is always there, can never be depleted and is equally accessible to all.

We need you to be that One that ushers in the new world of Love. Show your brothers and sisters the face of Love; they need someone who looks like them and is walking where they are presently walking. Hold their hand, remember why you have come and let Love lead the way.

On your planet love is defined or used three distinct ways. The first and the most widely used way is reciprocal love or ambivalent love. Webster's defines 'ambivalent love' as 'simultaneous conflicting emotions,' which translates into love with conditions. This is the love associated with I love you if. . . and you could proceed to write out the list of what someone must do, be and look like (You fill in the blanks.) for you to love them in this conditional exchange. And when they fail to fulfill your list, you no longer love them. Be honest, that is how most of you interact with the ones you love. But the ambivalent love is also interacted with everyone and everything. You love your car when it runs properly and have emotions other than love for it when it fails to perform.

The second, and a giant stride in your awakening process, is a holy love or a non-conditional love. This love recognizes that others are merely a mirror of themselves. When another loves you, this love is accepted and given back. When another offers something less than love, one also realizes that is a mirror of something inside of them that they have been previously unwilling to bring to the surface through their conscious mind.

With this type of love, you recognize your brothers or sisters have been kind enough to bring forth those repressed issues, and you now have the wonderful opportunity to remove those repressed issues that have lain buried within your subconscious mind. With those issues removed, this allows you to get closer to God. This also has another unique quality in that it removes the issues between yourself and all of your brothers and sisters. Thus the climbing of the ladder back to God takes some giant leaps.

We will now look at how one day all minds will express Love on your planet. First, notice how in the first two definitions of love we used the lower case "l" but in the final definition we will use Love with a capitol 'L.' This is the Love of God, which is the essence of your very being. You have simply forgotten that and are attaching your thoughts to a lower frequency than one of God's. This Love has no opposite, no contrast, and no degree. Therefore, the opposite of Love is Love. That really is beyond your understanding, and We are not asking you to understand certain concepts. We simply ask you to head in that direction by moving from ambivalent love to a Holy Love, and then God will take the final step for you."

Fusing Energy with Purpose:

"The fusing or merging of the energy of Love and your purpose are actually identical. If you are in alignment with who you are as a child of God you will know your purpose at every instant. Being in alignment with the energy of God is really being in your natural state of Oneness. So while you are working within your divine purpose, you are in alignment with the energy of God. And if you are in alignment with the energy of God, you will automatically be drawn to do what Love is guiding you to do.

119

*The Oneness frequency knows not of the egoic mind,
where its purpose is to repress your fears. And this false
purpose emanates from the illusion of you being capable
of aligning with something other than Love. We are trying
to teach you through contrast because that is the way you
presently live. With the ushering in of a new world,
contrast will vanish from your most holy minds."*

Vortex for Love:

*"Being a vortex of Love requires a great willingness to
give up your nothingness to have everything. Oh, We
know that makes little sense to the egoic mind which feels
it has to control everything to survive. But the giving up of
control is really the giving up of the illusion of control.
The only thing you have control over is your emotions!*

*You try and control things because you feel it will bring
you peace. In your false belief you believe this elusive
peace is the result of what the world has robbed from you,
thus you believe you must control the world in order for
you to be peaceful. What a daunting task to undertake,
having the sole responsibility to control the world. Even
the ego would have to wave the flag when one states it in
this fashion.*

*Being a vortex for love really is the only thing that is
natural. There is no need for sacrifice on your part. You
are not being asked to give up your dreams for the good
of others. Notice what we are asking you to be is a vortex
of Love. That is who you really are. We are only asking
you to recognize that part of you and let go of the thought
that that you must defend against some other truth of
whom you are.*

*When you say, 'I allow myself to be a vortex for the love
of God to flow through me. By this allowance I also help*

others to allow themselves to be a vortex for the love of God to flow through them.' In the application of this simple affirmation you are in alignment with who you are, who God is, who your brothers and sisters are, and thus open yourself up to receive all the good the Universal Giver of joy and happiness has in store for you. You will know who you are and your divine purpose.

With all the joy and happiness you will receive you will want to share it with the world because of the abundance you will have. Love has to be shared; it is in its nature. Living by example is the best teacher you can be for mankind. I cannot stress enough how important it will be for you to become this vortex for love. If there was only one thing I could say to you in this book that would be it. Become the vortex of love that you have been predestined to be. Once you have found that place inside of you then you are ready to help others to see that they too are this vortex of love."

Be that One!

Chapter 13: Honor, Compassion and Excitement

Anderson's Mantra:

Anderson's Mantra after his death was Honor, Compassion and Excitement and has continued to be so from right after his death through the writing of this book. I've inserted his first explanation of what this means and how it can be incorporated into your life so that you can realize the Anderson we knew, loved and will miss through the remainder of our lives:

> *"I came without a beginning and I have no end. I came to remind you of who you really are, to stop settling for and start accepting the unlimited joy your Creator has for you. I have come to bring you hope, and these words I leave with you: HONOR, COMPASSION and EXCITEMENT.*
>
> *Now go and bring a smile to someone's face, the person in the corner who's afraid to dance, dance with them. The child who takes on the appearance of being a nerd, make him/her feel as popular as you. When you play, play gently, stroke gently; and when you love, love gently. When you look into the eyes of your brothers and sisters, remember those three words I left you with: HONOR, COMPASSION, and EXCITEMENT. Open your heart and I will be there. You think I am gone but I am as close as your breath. From One who lives not in time, a joyful look back and a gentle smile. As always, your brother in Love, Anderson*
>
> *These are the three words I left you with at the Celebration for Life. I know tears still come to you as you write this, as it brings back memories of a past that still has a sting to it. Honor, Compassion, and Excitement are*

the dominant way you have lived your life since. Be proud of that, it can only bless you and those with whom you come into contact, be it personal or predominately to deliver these messages. If and when one looks at these words, I mean really look at these three words, there is much to notice there."

Honor:

"Honor is a word greatly misunderstood on your planet, and We do mean greatly. Honor is usually associated with honoring someone, something, or some organization. Another dominant way in which it is perceived is doing what the world defines as, 'The right thing to do,' or 'The honorable thing to do.' We are not saying one shouldn't do those things, but what we are saying is most do them for the wrong reasons. Different ways that honor comes forth on your planet entails the desire to please people, to feel important, to fit in with a certain group, to be liked by someone or by emulating ways one's ancestors did something, and many more. But the main reason is because someone or some organization has said it is the right thing to do. Notice, I use the word 'do.' 'Do' is associated with action. Honor needs only be associated with listening to the mighty Voice for Truth. And in this inner listening the doing will come forth and mirror honor.

The ego has a plethora of things that one must do to conform to its belief of what is right and wrong. This right and wrong strictly comes from a moral code of doctrines that are carved from fear. Funny thing about a moral code, it has constantly changed throughout time. What was morally right 100 years ago in certain situations is now morally condemned. Right and wrong always comes from the egoic mind emanating outwardly for the singular and self-proclaiming purpose of, 'I am the good guy because of the actions I have taken. And if I am the good guy, someone else must be the bad guy.' All this is based on the insane premise that there is this moral code that everyone has to follow, and those that do are put on the good side of the ledger, and those that don't are put on the bad side.

We are not saying what one should or shouldn't do. But based on a certain date and time on your planet, your gender, and what country your body is assigned will likely determine what is morally right within this honorable thing to do or say. If you do not conform your behavior within the defined boundaries your country has set up, you will be considered rather radical. These codes, and they can be subtle at times, permeate the whole planet. Notice how some people who lived earlier in history are later judged as great after they were not necessarily welcomed by the people of their generation. Just a few obvious examples are: Jesus, Gandy, and Martin Luther King are the most obvious ones, but there are literally thousands that have made enormous differences for others on your planet. Women will definitely take a lead in the future as their voice will now be welcomed. One such women that gets very little notoriety is Julia Ward Howe.

Honor is the way We would like you to interact with others in your life and is quite different from the way the world perceives. Honor is doing what the Voice for Truth is guiding you to do in that particular moment. There really is nothing We can tell you directly as to what you should do in any given circumstance. Even when faced with the exact same interaction, the Voice for Truth might guide you to do something entirely different the next time it comes into your awareness. The reason for that is, between the first interaction and the next encounter people change, and the Voice for Truth will always direct one's action so that both parties win. That is completely different than your ego, where it must always win. And

125

when there is a winner it will always be at the expense of the loser. And your ego is only concerned with appearances and this "looking good" equates to being the good guy.

To the degree that you are willing to want peace within this type of situation will match to the exact degree that you have heard the Voice for Truth. When that is happening, then you are honoring your true Self. The more one listens to this inner guidance, the more life will have a wondrous flow to it. You will no longer struggle to accomplish things: they just magically seem to unfold. When you need help, it will seem to come from the most unexpected sources at just the right time. And when you have honor, you will have compassion, and when you have compassion, you will have excitement."

Compassion:

"Compassion is another simple word that is greatly misperceived on your planet. Notice that I keep using the word 'simple.' Most of the words used throughout this book will be overlaid with a singular message that is designed to be understood in the most simplistic fashion possible. You make everything way more complicated than it needs to be. The message is simple, that what you project outwardly comes back to the receiver, so the world simply mirrors your thoughts.

This book is designed to have you really look at the world and notice how it makes you feel. If you don't like the feeling, you can choose another feeling about it, and the world will mirror that back to you. Once again, go inside and be honest with yourself, and you will see the ego has never truly made you happy. Only by doing what the Voice for Truth has offered will you be able to bring this elusive peace you are so desperately seeking into your life.

When one sees the emptiness of the offerings the ego holds out, one will naturally have compassion for themselves and their fellow brothers and sisters. Compassion on your planet usually comes from a place of fear, and thus if fear is in your heart, that is all you are capable of offering your brothers or sisters. Be honest! When someone you love or reminds you of someone you love, is facing a perplexing situation, then that can generate emotions of loss, hopelessness, or fear in you as well. And, because of where they are at that particular time, that also brings up fear in their life.

With you seeing this fear that you now have on your viewing screen, we need to ask you a question. How are you going to view what you are seeing? What We mean by that is, which voice will you listen to, the egoic voice that tells you to fix the event/person or the Voice for Truth which tells you to ask for your fear to be removed from what you are experiencing? If you listen to the egoic voice you will be coming from a place of fear, and all this experience can offer is fear in return. If the offering originated from the egoic mind, no matter how you dress it up, it will be always be overlaid with fear, and then at some future time this fear will come back to you.

If you ask the Voice for Truth to remove the fear which was generated within your most Holy mind from the event or person, what you offer will be coming from Love. And with this new offering, no matter how you dress it up, you will be coming from love. The offering has little to do with the healing of oneself or another, but what is of utmost importance is your motive. Be honest once again in your offerings. You will know if you are coming from fear or Love.

*Please don't judge what you have physically done,
caused, given or not given as something good or bad, but
only see the intent behind the offering. There will be times
when the egoic mind and the Voice for Truth will guide
you to do the same thing, but their results will be
drastically different. So, if your action comes from Love,
you have mastered the dynamics of* **Compassion;** *if not,
ask the Voice for Truth to help you."*

Excitement:

*We look and see how the word 'excitement' frightens
many of you. This thought emanates from various
reasons, but it is overlaid with a deep-seated feeling of
unworthiness. Of course, there are numerous others. I am
sure most of you could say that 'I have done things God
would not be proud of.' 'Excitement isn't holy, and
besides, I am trying to do what God wants me to do.' And
We would tell you Foolishness to such thoughts!*

*You list your emotions in categories, one side is good and
the other bad, and, unfortunately, excitement for the most
part is considered on the side of bad. If God is Love and we
are one with God, and this is true, then we are Love. If God
is Joy, and this is true, then we are Joy. If God is
Happiness, and this is true, then we are Happiness. Then
all this Love, Joy, and Happiness should instill Excitement
within you.*

*Have you noticed that when you feel connected you are
motivated and can really feel excitement deep within you?
Well, being spiritually connected can also bring up
feelings of excitement in all areas of your life. Many on
planet Earth only attach the word excitement to fun or
even sinful things. Please remember that your actions are
neither good nor bad, but merely the purpose you give
them. Give each interaction in your life a Divine purpose*

*and you can only feel the emotion of excitement to go
along with that.*

*Are you attracted to people who are excited about what
they do? You may not necessarily agree with what they
do, but you do admire them because they are motivated in
what they are doing. Let people see that listening to God
inspires you, and what you do is overlaid with
excitement."*

This Generation:

As Anderson spoke about in the first book, the current generation will
shepherd in a paradigm shift in consciousness.

> *"This generation will face issues that very few people can
> dream of at this present time. The WWII generation was
> called the Greatest Generation. But I tell you this
> generation will surmount all the previous ones. Time will
> show us this to be true. We look at the world of
> technology and see the lightning speed at which things
> change. What is the norm today is outdated as it is being
> printed. But the spirit of most seems to be stuck in the
> dark ages, where even the printing press is still but a
> dream. This will change!*

> *This generation will be the one that takes that quantum
> leap from holding onto the past to embracing their
> Greatness. This Greatness has nothing to do with
> overcoming worldly obstacles, but they will be able to
> overcome the self-imposed fears that lay buried in the
> subconscious mind.*

> *Their Journey will be inward. This generation will truly
> usher in the time of Peace that was spoken of many, many
> generations before. Remember there is only 'Love.' It has
> been a joy to be part of this unfoldment. Hold on, buckle*

up, enjoy the ride, the train has left the station. I have loved each of you with a love that has no end."

Science will help this generation in new ways. Because of the knowledge gained from various studies of the subconscious mind and how it operates, my generation will be able to explore inwardly in ways that past generations could not have dreamed of. They will be the ones that understand that it is their time to step up and BE THAT ONE! And in that realization they will accept that responsibility. They will work like no other generation before them to help bring this about. They will become the Vortex of Love that will LEAD their generation forward towards the Spiritual Actualization that was always the plan for mankind since the beginning of time."

Chapter 14: Evolving to Enlightenment

Gender:

"Energy is what you are and it has no gender. Since you believe you are either male or female this belief has split you off from your Source. This split has created duality in every aspect of your being. On your side of the veil on which your main attention is given, you will experience opposites on your planet. The veil and your attention to the dominant focus to one side of it will be discussed in greater detail in another chapter.

In this world of duality in which you believe you live, opposite thoughts within your mind must take form on your viewing screen and world. One of the forms it takes, and the seemingly dominate one, is the birthing of male and female. Our choice to come back and take on a bodily form is based on what the individual soul needs in this particular incarnation. These choices are made on the other side of the veil with your Spirit guides. Your purpose determines the choice of one gender over another. There are certain life lessons that can only be experienced in a particular gender. But one must keep in mind that everyone that has a body has both male and female cells in their DNA makeup. Your scientists have made it very clear that everyone has male and female cells.

Once again, since you believe you live in a world of opposites, you give everything a name. You see everything as separate with space in between each object. Therefore, you believe you have to give it a name. You feel you need

to study and examine it. You do everything to it except
love it. The naming of the separate genders is no different.

Similarly, many feel messages from above have to come in
a certain form or language or arrived via a certain
culture, and for some, via a certain gender. We will now
focus on love and how it is expressed through the
feminine gender on your planet. "

Male Dominated History:

"Just notice how your country, seemingly one of the most
open-minded countries in the world, still does a nice job
of forming division. This division can be subtle, but it still
serves the purpose of separation, and that is all your ego
is concerned with. Look how everyone lives, supposedly in
one united nation. But you have African Americans, Irish
Americans, Jewish Americans, Hispanic Americans, and
so forth. Then, you divide even further, male/female,
north/south, young/old, etc.

Why can't you just be Americans? That would be a way to
help bring people together. How can you come together
globally when you can't even come together in a single
country? Look at some of the indigenous tribes – they
came together as a singular tribe.

Women, in general, have had their voices silenced for
centuries on your planet. Because of this stifling of the
feminine voice, the energy of the planet has been tilted to
the masculine. This imbalance within the planet has
stunted your growth. But now women and their voices will
be heard in far greater numbers than at any other time on
the planet. There will be a swing towards hearing the call
from the feminine gender, and then a more balanced
approach to living in Love will present itself on your
planet.

Women have to accept these new roles in positions of power. We will not get into historical roles women have been ascribed to in the past. We are only concerned with NOW. Women have experienced things their male counterparts cannot, and because of this, they can express spirit in a way that most males lack. Remember, this energy is not strictly exclusive to one certain gender, but as a whole the world is currently opening up to hear these messages from the softer, feminine voice.

The masculine ways of winning at all cost have proven their leadership inept. They have played out these roles over and over again on your planet in every facet, and each time they have failed as have the ones before them. There are many people on your planet who have seemingly given up on life because of the way they see the world being governed. And by owning their blame, the males see they have been the ones with control, and so now there is distrust amongst all of the male species on this planet. Just look at the 'shotgun' approach they take regardless of how enlightened males are. Therefore, even if they are delivering a message of love, it simply will fall on distrusting deaf ears."

The Enlightened:

"An Enlightened being is the essence of one who no longer has any egoic thoughts. By far the vast majority of these entities are on the other side of the veil in a nonphysical form. There can be those in a body who have made the choice to come back in a bodily form to help the evolution of the planet.

As discussed in the chapter on the body, you are pure energy, and this energy not only permeates your body but everything on your planet, and it has no gender. Therefore, an enlightened being can have the appearance

133

of being a male or female, but not really be either. The choice of what sex you will be is solely based on what is best for the upcoming planetary shifts that will be taking place on your planet. In every religion, each race, and on every continent these enlightened beings are walking amongst us within these distinct demographics. These individuals, who chose to come to this planet while still evolving, are also trying to remember the Totality of Now. Their decision to incarnate in a male or female body is based strictly on what is best for that individual.

For an individual to reach that level of ascension, i.e., one who no longer has an ego, the individual must reach inside themselves to that part where they no longer see a difference between their needs and others and deeper yet until they see no difference between where they begin and God ends. Until that has taken place, their individual needs will outweigh their brothers' and sisters' needs, as well as your global needs on this planet.

Women, as a whole, are better equipped to express these messages than men. They have to accept their new power, and with this new power they must accept the associated responsibility. Most women have previously been unwilling to handle these situations. One mistake women have made in the past, and are still presently making, is they feel they have to be just like their male counterparts in order to make it in corporate America. Actually, some of them even feel they have to look like their male counterparts.

This newfound power brings temptations of the ego that must be confronted and contained. Some women will fail at first, as their male counterparts have, but most will remember how others have failed in the past and will choose differently. Because of this, most will honor their new leadership roles in numbers never seen before on this planet.

Some women may feel they have to express spiritual messages the way the old regime has done in the past. I must tell you 'Nonsense to such foolish beliefs.' In order to be heard you will have to present the messages differently that before. You must look at the problems and their solutions in a different way to be part of this paradigm shift. The world needs to hear the messages of peace, freedom, and reform from a voice that has compassion and love written over the messages. When this occurs, then people will listen, and in this listening a light will flicker from within, which will lead to self-reflection. This is what is needed to bring about the changes necessary for this planet to survive."

The Feminine:

"As always, your part is simply you need to ask for help in how you are to present these messages. You will need to act as a vortex for this love. Please don't say, 'Oh, I have given my power away to men, and now you are asking me to give my power away to God.' NO, please understand that your power is God's. You are God and there is no difference between you.

This surrendering of the ego can only be experienced with a deep feeling of love of which you have never experienced before. When Love guides your way, you will not be concerned with the views of others, nor consider being judgmental of other women holding power. You will know where your true power comes from, and you will not deviate from the part God has assigned for you.

The old female regime, with their antiquated views that still permeate your planet, will experience great difficulty with these changes. Many will not be able to accept their power, the power that comes from being in charge and in control. These women could possibly have made a decision on the other side to have chosen to incarnate in a female body because they didn't want control.

The world has stifled the feminine voice for so long and has associated the male species as having the ultimate authoritative voice of power. Males have had the scale tipped in their favor for the last two to five thousand years and have repressed women as a collective group. Thus, the name of God comes forth in the masculine form. In repressing the feminine voice, males have repressed their own energy of love that can only be expressed in that part of their heart that knows this feminine aspect of love.

To take the stifling process even further, those in authority have blocked the divine union of the blending of the male and female energies present in each of you. Women, that Divine aspect of Love, need to take the initiative in this blending of the two energies. It definitely will not come from the male species side the vast majority of the time. I am sure we don't need to go into how men do certain things and women do certain things. There is enough already written on that subject.

Women and society are now accepting of the feminine voice more. The presence of women in roles never imagined before is about to change and change at a rate never seen on your planet. Women will definitely acquire more power, but more importantly, they will be able to express love in a way that wasn't acceptable before. This will allow for the expressing of the alkaline blending of these energies where they were previously separated by those who were coming from fear. In referring to this blending of energies, we are speaking about the males/females, yin/yang energies and not necessarily, though not excluding, from a relationship perspective. This blending of energies needs to occur inwardly first, and then how it is expressed on your planet will become quite irrelevant."

Accepting the Feminine Power:

"For this paradigm shift to occur, women will have to take the lead role in accepting their part in its unfolding and helping to minimize the severity of the shift's collapse. Your roles are imperative. And the ones that cannot hear it from a female voice aren't ready to hear it at the present time. For many will not be able to hear the messages no matter how they are delivered. With Love in your hearts and God's guidance to lead you, We need you to be that One!

Before we go any further, the word 'power' is greatly misunderstood on your planet. Power in the way We speak of it has nothing to do with control. This power comes through the knowing who you are as a child of God and in your ability to express love without being concerned whether the world approves with a ten or disapproves with a one. The more you step into your power, the less you will need the approval of others to make you happy.

When women are allowed – actually a better phrase would be 'when women agree' – to accept their true role on this planet, then the next phase in the unfoldment can begin. As we just previously stated, true love on your planet is the blending of the male and female energy, but we have to first accept the equality of both. This is one of the major shifts that will be taking place on your planet. Once this shift occurs then this planet will be ready for the next step towards Oneness."

Duality: Blending Male and Female Energies:

"Before the blending of male and female energies can occur, the planet needs to see more women in power. The new generation will not only allow it, they will demand

women in power, just like a lost child demands its mother when he finally returns home. Neither energy is complete in and of itself but requires the other to complete itself. This is the ultimate expression of love on your planet, and that is, once again, accomplished by the blending of both energies.

Once equality between the sexes has been reached, a true blending of the male and female energy can emerge. Each of you has both the feminine and male energies in your DNA, and you will express these different energies at different times. When you block one of these energies from expressing its Divine purpose, the blending process is stifled. And this is the main cause of all health-related issues. Until we blend these energies, we are not fulfilling why we are here.

This is the primary reason for the discomfort most of you feel between the genders as you walk hand and hand on your journey to God. There are methods on your planet to initiate the blending of the ultimate marriage of the Totality of Now. Many of these methods originate from the East. Because of individuals allowing this shift to occur inwardly, the shift will also need to appear outwardly, and Mother Earth will be the blessed recipient of this union. You will see more and more couples on your planet, whether they are romantically connected or not, coming together to be the new teachers to usher in these planetary shifts.

If two people are coming together and are of the same gender but their purpose is the blending of these energies, their life's purpose is being fulfilled. This does not mean that they have to be in a relationship for this to happen. Two friends of the same gender can blend these energies as well if that is their intention. Embrace it, love it, allow it; ready or not, it is coming! As I have said before, 'Buckle up, enjoy the ride, the train has left the station.'

This Divine energy will choose the role based on what is best for the individual to complete his/her assignment in this chosen incarnation. In addition, We would like to point out that what is best for the individual, in this blending, is best for the planet. The mere fact that you are reading this book indicates that you have already been in the presence of such beings. Their appearances vary greatly. They come from all walks of life, all races, all religions, and cover all sexual preferences. Most have had numerous incarnations, but there are a few that have chosen to manifest on this planet for the singular purpose of helping others recognize their Totality of Now and have never tasted being in a physical body, but this is rather rare."

The impact of living a life in Oneness cannot be described with words.

Chapter 15: The Acceptance of Oneness

Being in Oneness:

"We love the way the section is titled: 'Being in Oneness.' That is because being in Oneness entails a feeling of Oneness and not a seeing of Oneness. Your eyes will never see Oneness because your sight is based on a dualistic thought system. Thus because of your dualistic thoughts, you will have to see a difference in everything and a space in-between each object.

That is why there will always be a good guy and a bad guy, victim/victimizer, hot/cold etc. You must ready yourselves for these shifts, and the help you will need to get through it will be provided. An opportunity is available to help you to shift from fear to love. Once you chose love over fear, your energy level will rise to become equivalent to the speed of the accelerated energy coming into the planet. Pain will motivate you to make this shift, but it is our hope that you make the internal shift coming from love. In making the shift coming from that place of all knowing, the shift will be relatively void of pain.

Raising your vibration to that of Oneness, for the vast majority of you, will be a process. Don't let the word 'process' fool you as you no longer have the luxury of time, as was the case for previous generations. With the luxury of time most people do very little because there is always tomorrow.

Given where you presently find yourself, most will learn through contrast. Because of the energy coming into the planet, the contrast of emotions will be magnified to just a

141

degree that the pain will motivate you. We are asking you to acknowledge that fear. Actually, we are asking you to embrace that fear. It is in the embracing of the fear, the feeling of empowerment lights up the mind. Now, you are in control of your life. Sounds strange, does it not? But with your ownership of your emotions you now have control over what to do with them. If you blame someone/something for your loss of peace, you are no longer in control of your emotions. The event or person will dictate to you how you feel.

With the acknowledgement that you have authorship of your feelings, ask yourself if you like this feeling. If the answer is no, then you have to give it to the Voice for Truth. The Voice for Truth will gladly remove them from your most holy mind. The singular purpose of the Holy Spirit is to help you remember who you are as a child of God, and every time you give the Holy Spirit an emotion other than love you are collapsing time. When you have sufficiently done this enough times, the shortening process of collapsing time becomes almost immeasurable. It is imperative that you ready yourself so when these shifts take hold, you will already be in a place of love. "

Practicing Our Oneness:

"When you are in Oneness, practicing it will be the easiest thing on your planet to do. The reason it will be this simple is that everything you will be doing will be coming from love, and the by-product of love is love. The most common feeling each of you will experience is a deep desire to share and to be of service to your fellow brothers and sisters.

The egoic mind equates everything to doing something. There is a part of the mind that would have you ask, 'What would a holy person do?' and then proceed to do

142

that. The action taken from a place of fear will want great fanfare in return for its shallow offering. The more you get in touch with your feelings, and your body is the base indicator at the present time, you will know readily whether your actions are coming from love or fear.

Practicing your Oneness entails giving of oneself to help others, but it also includes recognizing their Spirit Self at the same time. Each person on this planet is God and that includes everyone. You are all Divine spirits walking this Earth in a body, each with your own paths to traverse. You are all here to assist with each person's walk back to God and our Oneness."

Collapsing Time:

"For most on your planet, time is thought of and experienced in a linear fashion as past, present, and future. Actually, in reality, time is merely a continuous now, but we experience it in segments. With that in mind, we will explain it as you feel it. To collapse time one must step out of time.

This stepping out of time actually is done numerous times through the day. Every time you allow your mind to listen to the Voice for Truth you have stepped out of time. We create our pain in time, which means we have listened to the ego. And if you try to overcome the pain associated with these misaligned thoughts by further listening to this false self, you merely bury yourself deeper and deeper into a thought system that truly holds no way out. But when we listen to the Voice for Truth, we rise above these karmic laws and collapse time. What would have taken many lifetimes to work through an issue can be overcome with one act of forgiveness under the guidance of the Holy Spirit."

Hearing Our Messages:

"There are numerous ways of hearing the messages from those on the other side of the veil. There is no one way, nor is one way any better than another. What works best for you is how it will happen for you. If you need an audible voice, it will come that way. If you can only accept it though dreams, it will come that way. If you can only accept it through feelings, it will come that way.

Wake up each morning and set your intention of listening to the messages your loved one or Spirit Guides or Angels are trying to reveal to you on the other side. When you go to sleep at night ask them to be with you and reveal the messages they are so desperately trying to bring to you. There is nothing wrong with having your loved one come through another person to retrieve messages. In fact, if done properly, this will allow you to do the exact thing. The reason for this is it affirms in your mind they are truly there and their messages are of importance. When you have accepted this much, it frees you up to make your connection using the same modality as those on the other side.

As I mentioned in the first book, one way of making contact is to first center yourself and breathe deeply and slowly. Focus your attention on your breathing. One great thing about focusing on your breath is you have to be in the present during that focus. After about two minutes of steadily focusing on your breathing, say something in the order of, 'Hello, (Insert contact name) this is (Insert your name), 'Are there any messages you have for me at this time?' Then reverse roles and say as if you are the entity you want to contact, 'Hello, (Insert your name), this is (Insert contact name),' and then just wait silently for the messages.

The mere fact that you have asked requires a response. If you feel you haven't received anything, please don't view this as a failed attempt. There are numerous reasons for not being able to hear the messages he/she is trying to give you. Some of which are: trying too hard, or you feel the messages need to come in a certain form, or you feel you already know the answer and just want the person to validate your 'knowing,' or you are coming from your false religious beliefs . . . The reason really does not matter, as there are numerous other reasons for not allowing the messages to come forth on this side of the veil.

Know that if you have asked, then the answer is there waiting for you to be still enough to hear the message. Be aware that when you least expect it the message can come forth, so be on the lookout because it will come. You have beckoned, and their soul will respond. Take note that there will be times it will come forth when you are doing "mindless" things, like washing dishes, mowing the yard, reading the paper, etc. because that is when your ego is quiet.

The second method we would like to set forth is receiving the messages during your dream state. Set the intention before going to sleep by saying something in the order of, 'I would like to make contact with (Insert contact name) and I give (Insert contact name) full authority during my sleeping state to bring forth messages from the other side.'

When you awake you may or may not remember the messages, but, once again, if you have asked for a response, then it has to be forthcoming. It is easier for you to hear messages from those on the other side of the veil in your waking state than your sleeping state. So right when you awaken in the morning, ask for your awareness to be one with your loved one, and be open to receive the messages he/she is trying to bring forth. Once again, this 'half-awake' state as opposed to your sleeping state is more conducive to hearing messages.

*The third way, and there are others that will be brought
forth in later books, is receiving the messages from
another person, books, movies, emails, etc. Most people
on your side of the veil are extremely fearful of actually
hearing from us on this side of the veil. Therefore, we will
reach you by any means that you allow us to get these
messages across. Books, other people, etc., are less
fearful to most, so We will use these as well as numerous
other methods to give you guidance from across the
unknown sea.*

*There are two very important intervals throughout the day
where it is more conducive to access your subconscious
mind. Actually, I have heard certain modalities on the
planet use the words: Super-conscious Mind, Source or
Source energy as synonymous with God. It is funny how
people seem to go out of their way not to use the word
God. But your subconscious mind is actually connected to
the God part of the mind.*

*We would highly recommend before you go to sleep to
settle the mind and end your day by declaring it over,
finished, done and forgiven. Then ask right before going
to sleep to be guided by (Insert contact name.) in what
you are to do when you awake in the morning. Then when
your body awakens in the morning, you have a very short
interval of time where you are consciously awake but
your mind is still connected to the subconscious mind.
This is probably the best time to access information that
needs to be carried out on this side of the veil. This does
not mean these are the only times you can connect to your
Source, but morning and evening are definitely the most
conducive times during the day, given where most of you
are on the path back to God.*

*When you settle your mind at the end of the day, ask for
guidance from whatever higher Source of Love that you
perceive guides you. This does not always mean that your
dreams will not be overlaid with fear. You have taught*

*yourself on this planet that fear is bad and that fear is to
be avoided. You also believe that fear means you have
done something wrong. Or even more deeply buried in
your subconscious mind, you believe you are a bad
person, guilty as charged, or even deeper, unworthy of
God's Love. Your subconscious is like a storage bank that
holds information that can be accessed at any time. And
that is true, but in the storage bank there is virtually every
piece of information that is available to all.
Unfortunately, most merely seek out the information to
defend whatever particular thoughts your ego presently
holds.*

*By asking your Higher Power to reveal your purpose in
life, which is in the storage bank, before going to sleep,
you can actually unlock the answers you have been
desperately seeking. In order for you to hear the answers
to your questions, you have to remove the interference of
unwanted files so the Voice for Truth can help you to
remove these unwanted files of fear. Your dream state is
actually the most desirable place for that to occur.*

*What you call nightmares is at times the Voice for Truth
bringing these fear files up so they can be removed. Not
all nightmares fall into this category, but most do. This is
actually good because you already know in your
subconscious mind that you are one with Spirit and what
your purpose is in this incarnation. But you have to clear
out the plethora of thoughts that block your heart's
desires from being fulfilled. Remember before going to
sleep to ask the Voice for Truth to remove your unwanted
files and thoughts that can be brought up during your
sleeping state.*

*When you have a dream that frightens you, be grateful
that these undesirable thoughts that you have buried in
your subconscious mind are now in the forefront of the
mind so they can be removed. The removal process is
rather simple. First one must own those feelings and not*

147

*judge them. Then you need to realize they no longer serve
a purpose and send unconditional love to them. Then give
the frightening dream over to the Holy Spirit, or whatever
name you want to use for your higher power. Then the
Voice for Truth can remove those unwanted dreams or
thoughts and replace them with thoughts that will make
your heart sing.*

*In addition, you can ask the Voice for Truth to provide
you with very specific instructions on how to carry out
what you are supposed to do each day. The Voice for
Truth's instructions are very action oriented, and, as
such, you will be asked to do what is in your highest and
best interest for that day. These instructions are meant to
guide you in your purpose for being here.*

*There is a big misconception that Spirit is very passive.
Nothing could be further from the Truth. When you are in
Spirit you are inspired and will want to take action. The
action coming from Spirit is different than action coming
from the egoic mind. Action stemming from your egoic
mind might ultimately mirror the same action stemming
from Spirit, but taking the action is really unimportant.*

*It is the purpose you give the action that will produce
either love or fear within your life. Action taken from
Spirit will inspire you, your body will be healthier, your
relationships will be more harmonious, and your
monetary flow will bring you greater peace. When action
originates from your egoic mind, your body will feel
restricted, your relationships will be unfulfilling, and you
can never have enough money to make you happy."*

Messages as Dreams:

*"You people on planet Earth look at dreams solely as
occurring when you are asleep. During your sleeping*

state, dreams are usually classified into nightmare or happy dreams, but because you have labeled your sleeping dreams unreal you give them little attention. Nightmare dreams are good in that when you awake you know they are just a dream and usually dismiss them rather easily.

Your mind never sleeps; it is on duty twenty-four hours a day, seven days a week and three hundred and sixty-five days a year. When you have egoic thoughts while awake, the law of cause and effect or karmic laws come into effect. Actually, they come into effect while you are asleep too, but the ease with which you dismiss these dreams lies solely in the belief of their illusionary state. Because of this you stop the law of cause and effect and karmic laws from being activated from your dreams.

Your ego is just a computer with a plethora of files, most containing untruths of your true nature. Whether you go through the process of removing those unwanted files during your waking hours or sleeping hours makes no difference. But, once again, while you perceive a difference between your seemingly illusionary sleeping thoughts and your waking thoughts, your sleeping thoughts will be easier to release because you have already defined them as unreal.

Given the illusionary nature you have given your sleeping thoughts, you should view your waking thoughts in just the same manner. Your sleeping thoughts and waking thoughts are equal in nature, and with this recognition the removal process will become much easier. The projection of all thoughts emanate solely from two distinct sources in your mind, the egoic part and the 'Voice for Truth.' When you arise in the morning and your recent dream thoughts have brought up fear to your awareness simply say, 'That was a dream. It is unreal. I choose Love instead of these thoughts. You could also say, 'It was only a dream. There is only love,' or 'This moment is perfect in time. I choose to extend Love in this Moment.'

Throughout the day, whenever a thought comes to mind that produces an emotion other than love say, 'This is a dream. It is unreal. I choose love.' Or 'This moment is perfect in time. I choose to extend love in this moment.' Notice how, once again, the above two paragraphs are basically the same. The reason I say this is based on the fact that the sleeping and waking thoughts are identical. At the deepest level our sleeping dreams are really our subconscious mind trying to bring forth either needed information or thoughts that need to be cleared. Do not brush aside your dreams; they can contain valuable information for you. In the future your scientists will be able to prove the previous sentence correct.

Actually, a lot of psychic information can come from dreams. But you must give dreams a divine purpose, because dreams can also come forth from the egoic part of the mind. Set the tone before bed by asking for guidance in your dream state. Write down your dreams, and you will see your dreams are a virtual road map to your future.

I am still amazed by how people are still so afraid of their dreams, even those who have read the first book. Most of your dreams are your subconscious thoughts being brought to the conscious mind. At times during the day when you can still your mind long enough, the subconscious can bring forth added insights to you. Perhaps you have asked a question and at the same moment the answer comes to you. For most people in the West this seems rather difficult because they are so used to keeping their mind active and doing things. But when they do what you might call "mindless" things, like mowing the lawn, washing dishes, sitting in your car waiting for someone, the subconscious at times bleeds through and you are able to access your higher thoughts.

Notice how we refer to a veil between the seen and the unseen, between form and formless. Between the conscious mind and the subconscious mind there is also a barrier. This barrier is just like the veil between those that still presently walk this planet and those that have laid their body down. Your subconscious mind is readily available for your viewing if you will just lay aside your judgments about yourself and others. Its choices will always come back to the simple question of 'What is of the highest and best benefit for me?' If your only goal is that of extending Love, you will automatically have access to the part of your mind that seems to lay buried deep within.

We will point out that the ONLY reason for you not wanting to have a singular goal of extending love is because you believe love will ask you to give up something that you like. It is written all through your religions. Look at Lent and your reciprocal relationships. Look at how you acquire things. It is all based on either having to give something or give up something to get something; is it not?

Love, which is the essence of who you are, asks nothing of you. What could it possibly ask? You already have everything. Love has everything, and you are one with Love. Ponder on that awhile!"

Meditation:

"There are countless ways to meditate, and, strictly speaking, every thought centered in love is a meditation regardless of the physical stance, position of eyes, or any mantra that might be spoken. What I am going to focus on is what form of meditation will be most beneficial for you to unleash your psychic potential. I am not saying other forms of meditation are not helpful, they are. Nor am I

saying that this is the only way to meditate, as every form of meditation is helpful. Remember, prayer is a form of meditation, although most don't look at it in that way. Because of the urgency of time on your planet, we have given you the fastest way to unleash your psychic abilities.

For this reason, your meditation needs to focus on the going inward, deep into the Mind and Heart of God. Remember, if you are to use your psychic talents to bring forth love to a world in dire need of love you must become love. You no longer have the luxury of talking about love, seeking love, referring to love, studying love, etc. You must become the embodiment of love. And one of the tools that would benefit you is the meditation of going deep into the Heart and Mind of God.

Mentally watch your breathing; watch it come in and watch it go out. Do that for a few minutes and while staying focused, use a mantra afterwards, something like, 'Love,' 'Om,' or 'God.' You need to use a mantra that resonates with you, but keep it short. One-word mantras work nicely, but you can use a longer one if you want. We will give the definition of a mantra as 'anything said over and over with the singular purpose of helping you make contact with that divine part of you.' Do this for a minimum of five minutes each morning and evening. Feel free to do it longer than five minutes if you are so inclined."

Chapter 16: The Purpose for Being Here

Our Purpose for Being Here:

"We will not discuss your path that was chosen for you prior to you being here as we have discussed that in a previous chapter. What we will do is simplify it for you. Your purpose for being here on this planet is singular in nature. You are here to be a vortex for the Love of God to flow through you. How and what that will looks like will be highly individualized for each person. Being a vortex for love does not require you to give up your individual needs and wants because at a spiritual level individuality does not exist. When you are a vortex you have become part of the Whole. You will still have desires and needs but the fulfilling of them will be of benefit to all. The joy in accepting your part in this glorious unfoldment is literally indescribable – it can only be experienced. Be that One!

With this newfound love and purpose in your heart, all areas of your life will bring you such joy your heart will be unable to contain it all. We mean that literally. As the joy becomes so large, it has to be shared, and the sharing of it adds to your joy. Because of this abundance of joy, you will also seek out ways to help your fellow brothers and sisters discover it as well. And since you have found out who you are as this glorious child of God, you will want to remind them that they too are that same wondrous joyful child of God."

How Others May Perceive You:

"When you accept why you are here and acknowledge your purpose, then you are embracing who you are as a child of God. Once you have done that, then people's perception of you will have no bearing on how you feel. It is only when you are not comfortable with who you are that other people's views of you can have any bearing on how you feel about yourself. When you have accepted your part in ushering in a new world, those that have accepted their role will also recognize you. Those that still remain in the dream state will believe you are still like them.

The reason for those two groups, with their drastically different views of you, lies in the law of perception. Your laws of perception dictate that one must look inside and project that belief outwardly and then believe what their eyes and ears report back to it are true. Thus, everyone will have a certain picture of you based on what they need you to be. Be that One that allows your brothers and sisters to see the face of Truth when they see you. It is time to stop talking about love, analyzing love, and start being the embodiment of love. When a truly sufficient number of those in alignment with Love embrace their purpose, this embracing will alter the scale for those who remain asleep."

As I Teach I Learn:

"Teaching and learning seem to be two separate aspects that get played out in your interactions between yourself and others. You have trained yourselves to be very good at pointing out errors in others but seem to be unable to see the same errors within yourselves. One only needs to understand the 'mirror' principle to see that what we see in others is what actually lies inside our subconscious

mind. The egoic part of our mind never lets us understand that because of the dynamics of egoic projection.

What we want you to realize is what you see in others can only be seen because it is also an aspect of your own persona. Usually, the degree of discord in which you view and magnify what is in another appears so disproportionate to you that you can hardly see that it is also inside of you. But if what the person has done bothers you, you can take it to the bank that to some degree you would do the same thing to them or another.

But what is of the uttermost importance, and especially at this time in the unfoldment of your planet, is that you watch what advice you would give that person to correct their misdeeds. Whether you give them the advice or not is irrelevant. What is important is what you think they should do in their life to straighten them out is what YOU need to do. So thank them for pointing it out to you and thank yourself for realizing it too. So now you can choose again.

By far this is the best way the Holy Spirit can reach most of you because you are still unwilling to look inside first. If you think one should meditate more or think before they speak, please realize the other person is merely crying out for help. You should handle them with care as that is also exactly what you need to do in your life. We are not saying the other doesn't need to do those things too, but the message is always first directed to the messenger. In the offering of the message to another, one can only accept it with love for themselves first before showing up as the messenger."

Manifesting Your Dreams:

*"There is so much made of the words 'manifest' and
'manifesting your reality' like it is something new. The
moment the mind made a body the manifestation process
began. In fact, the projection of the body was the first act
of manifesting. And manifesting will continue to happen
for you even after you lay this body down. When you lay
the body down, your mind still is in the process of
manifesting something. It is incapable of not manifesting
something, and that is your true nature. While you are in
a body your only choice is whether you are going to
manifest from the fear-based perspective of your egoic
mind or from love by listening to the Voice for Truth in
your Spirit Mind.*

*The Christian words 'Spirit' and 'Soul' at some level can
be interchanged with the word 'Mind.' We are aware that
people can twist words and make them different than their
original meaning or, better yet, how the word is typically
interpreted on your planet. Whenever you are coming
from Love, the manifestations of your mind/spirit will
always bring joy to the giver and receiver. When it
emanates from the egoic mind, one will lose and one will
win. There is no exception to this spiritual law.*

*Every thought produces something on your planet. Look
outside and see what your planet is showing you. It can
only show you your thoughts. The world is the
manifestation of thoughts, nothing else. Therefore, if you
don't like what you see in the world, you can change it by
changing your thoughts. The world isn't good, nor is it
bad; it is simply the manifestation that mirrors back to
you your inward thoughts.*

*All words on your planet have various meanings, so what
we are doing here is trying to give words that you have
attached certain meaning to a different meaning.
Different professions or trades use the same word but*

156

they give it different meanings. The word 'run' to a painter means something different than to a baseball player. The word 'mouse' means one thing to someone on a computer but means something entirely different to a bug exterminator. Therefore, within the framework of this book you are going to have to give the words the meaning we have assigned to them in order to understand the messages being brought forth.

Manifesting, like everything else, is neither good nor bad, but the purpose one gives the reason for wanting to manifest something is extremely important. Once again, the purpose is the key to understanding what is going on currently in your life. I know we have stressed this before, but it is the key to understanding these messages and allowing your life to unfold in a gentle, loving fashion.

Most people on the planet manifest coming from fear; therefore, regardless of what they manifest, if fear is the thought behind the manifestation, the new manifestation will eventually produce fear. At first it may not seem that way, but once it is played out, one can recognize the fear behind the original manifestation.

If one manifests something coming from love, whatever the form, that new form will produce love. You cannot help but manifest, so the question should always be, 'Where am I coming from with this thought about manifesting what I desire?' Again, your purpose for the manifestation will determine your outcome of either moving away from fear or moving towards love.

When first trying to manifest something, most of you will start from a fear-based mode. Be honest, usually you want something because in the having of it, you believe you will feel better. If where you are at the present moment isn't bringing you the joy that makes your heart sing, then you need to consider alternative thinking. Most of you will believe the acquiring of the person/object will make you feel better, and there is nothing wrong in this wanting. In fact, you have to want things in this world as it is a world of needs. But if you ask the Voice for Truth 'What do I need?' the attainment of that response will always bring you joy. And in that asking, it will also be given to you, because the Voice for Truth always gives; it is in its nature. When asking from a place of fear, it doesn't mean you won't acquire what you are seeking, but in the acquiring of the person or thing you seek, it cannot give you the same level of joy you could have received coming from love. Watch how the manifestation from fear will eventually produce less then loving results.

Change your manifestation thoughts to 'I am loved,' with no fear around it. See mental images of you and your loved one(s) enjoying each other, loving and having fun. Know and trust absolutely that this will happen for you. These are the thoughts what will manifest what you are seeking. The end result of these manifestations is pure joy."

Our Relationship to Money:

"Money is energy and our thoughts are energy. Money is modulating at a certain vibrational frequency, and that degree of frequency is different for everyone. So when one raises their frequency, the flow of money has to increase. Now, on your side of the veil it may not show up as actual money in the bank, but what may show up is more of what the money represented to you. So if money means more free time to do what your heart has been calling you to do, the universe will arrange everything in your life for that to happen.

Be honest and ask yourself, 'What does money represent to me?' Notice how We started out the sentence, 'Be honest.' What does money represent to me?' If it is not in

*alignment with your higher power, more money will not
bring you the joy you think it will. When you give your life
the purpose of extending love, what money represents to
you will have to increase. There is a saying on your
planet, 'Do what your heart says and the money will
follow.' There is much truth to that statement.*

*Please watch how you use money and how you spend it. Is
there fear associated with the going out of money in your
life? If so, fear will return back to you as some point.
From a practical perspective, when you give money, give
it with love, and see the receiver with the money. It might
be your utility company or an ex-wife. And the next step
We would ask is for you to see them benefiting from the
exchange. When you are able to see the benefactor of the
money receive the money and know they are benefitting
from the money, then you have given money a divine
purpose. It is important not to judge any part of these
thoughts as that would not give it a divine purpose.*

*As most topics discussed in this book, energy and purpose
will play an imperative part is explaining each topic. For
money to appear in your life, it will first have to appear
as a thought in your mind. Thoughts have energy, and this
energy emanates from one of two sources. The two
sources that dwell within your mind are either The Voice
for Truth or your egoic or false self. If the manifestation
of money on your planet comes from the egoic false self,
then it will have fear wrapped around it. These fear
thoughts will restrict the flow of money and the joy it
could have brought forth. If you manifest money coming
from the part of your mind that is in constant
communication with your Creator, then your
manifestation of money will flow more freely and also
bring great joy into your life.*

*Everything on your planet is a mirrored representation of
something that you have at one point identified within
your persona. Money is no exception. Money represents*

different things to different people. Ask yourself 'What does money represent to me?' Be honest, because if you downplay your desires their manifestation will lay dormant. Then ask yourself 'How am I using money in that area of my life?' How you use money in that area will determine the restriction or open flow of money in your life. Once again, what purpose are you giving money is how it will manifest in your life.

We want to stress this very strongly; money is just ENERGY. Energy has to be fed, and your attention is that feeding energy. So when you focus on the purpose of your money that is also creating energy around the money. More importantly pay attention to whether or not your thoughts about money are positive or negative. This focusing is the fuel that will propel exactly what you are presently focusing on. If one is focusing on lack, lack will follow. If you focus on the benefits of the money then you will be coming from love.

Thought is energy. Energy manifests from thought. Energy creates your outcome from each thought. That is the LAW. Neither you, nor anyone on your planet, can change a Spiritual law. No matter how you try, you cannot change the law of gravity. Spiritual laws cannot be circumvented nor denied, no matter how much effort you put forth to overcome them.

The avoidance of money is virtually impossible on your planet. It is the means by which things are exchanged. Even if you went back to the bartering/exchange system, everything I am speaking about would still be applicable. Once again, remember money is energy, and energy is really just a thought. Therefore, thoughts cannot be avoided. Energy cannot be avoided; thus the attention you place on things or people cannot be avoided. Embrace your thoughts. Give attention to what makes your heart sing first of all and then the money will flow. It truly never works by putting money first and then your dreams.

Dream first then expect the money to show up to bring them into reality. Know that you deserve it.

We are really trying to have you get in touch with your feelings. Feelings are your true indicators as to which voice you are listening to at any given moment in time. If you are experiencing a feeling of joy then you are listening to the Voice of Love. Once you feel this joy then extend it out to increase joy everywhere. Notice that all feelings of joy have one thing in common. The common thread that permeates this feeling of joy is that it must go forth and be shared.

In other words, on your planet the going-forth means you will want to share joy with everyone. That is an aspect of your Love, the desire to share it with your brothers and sisters. What the form looks like in sharing joy is always highly individualized for the one choosing the emotion of joy. On the other hand, if one does not share what one has been given from the Spirit, one will block the flow of what generated that feeling to begin with, and in this analogy one will also block the flow of money into their life.

Hopefully, you have seen another characteristic of the egoic mind, and that is, when you receive an idea or emotion stemming from the egoic mind, you will want to hold onto those feelings, and the things these feelings produce in your life. In this example of egoic money, you would want to hoard what you have and believe the flow is limited. Your feelings are always your best indicator as to which voice you are listening to. Again, these types of limiting egoic thoughts always block the unlimited flow that would have been yours if you had been coming from a position of sharing joy.

The approach to bringing all that you desire into reality is based upon the following steps:

1. *Your thoughts: Hold a conscious intention for what it is that you want to manifest.*
2. *Hold your Divine purpose around the receipt of the item. (How you are going to lovingly use what you desire.)*
3. *Focus on having received it. Think, act and know that it is already yours.*
4. *Engage your actions to bring it forth into reality. Move in the direction of having already received it with all of your associated actions in alignment.*
5. *Let go and let God and the universe bring it to you.*
6. *Be completely accepting and aware of how and when it comes to you. Not all gifts appear as they were originally requested.*

Be kind to yourself on this subject. If the joy and money is coming from God, you would never have to experience an overdrawn statement on your account. And if your account is tied to your egoic mind, it will always be in the red. You need merely change how you look at it and choose again."

Chapter 17: Preparing for the Coming Shifts of Energy

Mother Earth and Planetary Shifts:

"Since the early 1990s the energy coming into your planet has been steadily increasing, but between 2012 through late 2015 the amount of energy coming into the planet will accelerate at a rate never seen before. This energy, as we describe it, is all good. But the good feelings intended for all will not be felt that way by the many who are unprepared. For those who are unaware and not ready to change from the old ways of interacting with themselves, their brothers and sisters, and planet Earth, this energy is going to feel like a disconnect.

Because of this disconnect, those unwilling to change their thought system will experience an increase in fear, and this collective fear could potentially produce some rather catastrophic events on your planet. Nothing, and we mean nothing is carved in stone. Nor is there any timetable as to when these potential negative events could occur. But shifts are definitely going to happen. What we can say with much certainty is there will be a shift in the way you interact with your brothers, sisters and Mother Earth. If the shift cannot be done in a gentle unfoldment, then those in fear will experience an unpleasant self-imposed shift. These self-imposed shifts should eventually guide people to start acting in a way that is in alignment with the ushering in of a new world of love.

We want to state that there will be no specific references as to what exactly will occur, nor will there be any dates mentioned. First, we want to express very clearly that what will take place on your planet has absolutely

163

nothing to do with the wrath of God. God is pure love, and, as such, the only thing that can flow forth from God is Love. Any negative events that could occur would be the outcome of the negative thoughts and emotions occurring at that time on your planet.

Any changes to your planet would be hard to specify because you, as a collective group, can choose to change your thoughts to Love, and with that shift to love, you will be able to alter what would have taken place. The severity and timing of these shifts can be altered by the energy created by your collective loving thoughts. Because your planet's collective consciousness constantly fluctuates between love and fear thoughts, any changes would be adjusted accordingly.

Your vibrations of Love send out energy which is of a much higher frequency than fear. Your scientists can tell you that in a scale of 1000, love vibrates at a relative frequency of approximately 500, and fear vibrates at a level of 100. The vibration of love unifies, but the frequency of fear polarizes. That is why it is imperative that you get yourself in alignment with who you are as a child of God. Not only so that you can go through these shifts with little or no difficulty, but because of the imperative importance in helping those that are going to experience a great deal of discomfort when the various shifts start to unfold on your planet.

The majority of your Bible is actually written in code. Because some of the codes can now be unraveled, people will be able to see and understand some of the events that will be taking place shortly. But even those predictions are subject to change based on the collective consciousness of the planet. There will be no apocalyptic events, but a gentle unfolding of peace for everyone. But this 'gentle' unfoldment will not necessarily be welcomed by everyone because of their particular investment in keeping things aligned with special interests. But this time *there will be nothing powerful enough on your planet to change what is about to unfold.*

Your normal way of interacting with others, your body, the way you work, and the way you normally view everything will have to change. For most, even the normal way of living in single family dwellings will change drastically. Communal living will become much more prevalent. At first some will choose communal living out of pure economic necessity. Later, as more and more of you drop the need to possess things, this type of living will hold much attraction.

Not that possessing things is bad. It is not. But what is detrimental is how these things are tied to your self-identification. During this timeframe is when more and more of you will start to realize that things don't determine who you are. Owning or not owning things does not make you any more or less. Actually, what makes you more or less, and by 'more or less' we are referring to more of the ego or less of the ego, is the dropping of your attachment to things. Those types of feelings are always constantly running from one end of the fear/love spectrum to the other, all of them based on external happenings. Not because possessing things is harmful or negative, it is because in and of themselves they are merely inanimate objects, but the identification with them is what will be laid aside by more and more of you.

As these paradigm shifts are being birthed, a new you will emerge. Your 'birthing' may be painful at times, but the results will be well worth it. All one has to do is ask the mothers on the planet. They endured bodily changes through pregnancy, then the pain of birth, but all was worth it because you had been the vortex for another soul to appear in human form.

Because of their understanding of birthing, women must play a pivotal role during these shifts. Because of the inherent ability to birth, whether they have done so or not, most women will go through these shifts in better shape than their male counterparts. Unfortunately, most women on your planet have never taken on any type of leadership role and will be hesitant to step forward to assist others. We ask that women grab that role with Honor, Compassion, and Excitement. The world will need your hands, your voice, and your ears to assist them through this process. Be that one!

In this new alignment with the Totality of Now, listening to sounds, vibrations, and certain types of music will assist those experiencing any one of the vast emotions one might go through during these shifts. Both classical and meditation music would assist in relieving any pressure or uncomfortable feelings associated with the shift. Even those that are allowing the shift to occur would benefit from certain types of sound-healing techniques that are available on your planet. Also mantras can have a very similar effect on those experiencing emotional discord during these shifts. There are also other modalities circulating around your planet which can help you in contacting those that have passed over to the other side of the veil, who can assist you as well.

In the West the mind isn't as disciplined as it needs to be. You love the word 'multi-tasking,' as if you really have accomplished something; but, in actuality, you have given little attention to either. You need to learn how to focus, and how to concentrate on one thing at a time. Be honest with yourself; when you are doing something you really love you can really focus your attention. And when something brings you great bodily enjoyment you know you can focus on the subject matter at hand. When you lump things together to accomplish them, you are telling your mind that these things are not important, and therefore your brain can discard them.

This might sounds a little strong but that is how the mind operates. It is quantitative; it literally weighs each emotion and judges them accordingly. This is all done within the egoic part of your mind, but in reality, it is only capable of two choices. One is Love and the other is fear, and in any given instant you can only be in one or the other emotion. And in choosing one you have to discard the other. So concentrate your thoughts on Love during the shift and by doing so you will come through joyfully.

Everyone has heard, 'The past in a good indicator of the future.' We will now tell you such thoughts are very destructive and they permeate your planet. It is the reason nothing much has changed from past generation to generation. When people are tied to the past and allow past actions or thoughts to dictate their future, there is little opportunity for change. There is some truth to that but only if you are tied to your ego. Please remember that within your egoic thought system there is no way out of this pattern. It is in the process of constantly trying to pay off its past karmic debts and within that thought system you can never pay enough. You past will truly equal your future within this type of thought system.

The primary purpose of your ego is to keep you tied to the past. If you are tied to the past then your mind is still trying to 'atone' for your guilt and will never have the time to be in the Now, which is where God is. You truly can never pay off your karmic debts within the egoic mind that has made the guilt. But the ego cleverly holds out another false option to you, and you'll try once more. The only way out of that thought system is to make a different choice of where to originate your thoughts, and that is through your spirit self and loving Voice of Truth. Remember to choose again.

During this paradigm shift, someone has to be willing to step up to provide others with a completely different way of interacting within themselves, others, God, and Mother

Earth. This cannot be done in small increments any longer. The planet does not have the luxury of time any more. In history every time your planet has been presented with alternative small shifts in energy, those on Earth merely readjusted it to and continued on with their old patterns of destruction.

I know the word 'destruction' seems rather strong here, but we have meant it to be that way. There is no gray area within the mind. The mind only has two options in which to choose to think from: the egoic mind or your spirit mind and Voice for Truth. We are trying to show you what has really been taking place within your mind and the results of your choices up until now. Hopefully, when one sees the insanity of what the ego has to offer, one will naturally make the only other alternative. These feelings of the Earth actually being destroyed are simply mirrored thoughts from within. For Mother Earth can only experience an earthquake as the result of people on the planet personally experiencing an emotional upheaval.

It will take relatively few of you who are in alignment with love and your true purpose on this planet to change the outcome for everyone. I'm sure most minds will think 'How can a few miracle-minded people change the world? That doesn't seem like a majority to me.' In looking at the word 'majority' one must ask the question, 'A majority of what?' The answer is a majority of energy, and energy can be weighed and measured.

Energy and purpose are the keys to understanding this book and all the messages it holds. A relatively small group of people who see their singular purpose is to help in the awakening process can have a collective energetic weight that outweighs the majority of everyone else on the planet. Therefore, they are the majority.

To explain this I will provide an example. Assume that the collective energy of everyone on your planet has a total numerical value of 1,000 points of frequency and there are 1,000 people on the planet. Now, if everyone vibrated at a measurement of one, then you would need 501 people to be a majority. Now I am sure you have come across people in various stages in the awakening process. These individuals that have dropped the need to be right, the need to control, and have remembered why they are here; they will register at a much higher vibrational frequency than one. So let's say, within the above analogy, that you have eight people who have been tested and register at a frequency value of 50, (a total of 400) and one that registers at a value of 101, (new total is 501) whatever thoughts they hold would then be the majority. There is virtually an endless number of mathematical ways to come up with a majority. Be that one that tips the scale!

That is why in talking to my father I usually end each conversation with, 'Be that One. Love, Anderson.' We ask you NOW to BE that One! What we can say with great confidence is there are going to be great changes coming to your planet, in greater proportion and speeds never experienced before on your planet. We can also say with a great deal of confidence is that all these shifts are not only good for you, but good for everyone else on this planet, as well as Mother Earth. Once again, when they start occurring, the changes will produce various reactions for most people. Some may even predict the world is coming to an end. But hear them not. Be that One that knows the purpose and understands your role in the transition.

These shifts are designed to be done in a gentle fashion, but how they occur will be determined by the ones perceiving the shifts. If one is attached to the old egoic ways of interacting on this planet, then these shifts will bring about a great deal of discomfort. But if one just allows these shifts to unfold and recognizes the joy behind each shift, then this experience will have no parallel. Your reason for being here will open up before you and give

*your life a completely different purpose. This new
awareness will allow you to look upon your brothers and
sisters with a love not previously conceived of before.
Welcome these shifts, embrace them, and the duration of
any discomfort once they start occurring will collapse for
you.*

*One reason for this fear of change is that most people
sleepwalk through their life and generally do as your
leaders ask of you. When they change the laws, you
accept that as a natural occurrence. You don't mind this
because when you know what to expect, there really is
very little energy involved in accepting the change
because you would have already made provisions for
what your leaders have assigned. Some of your leaders
already know these events are coming, but because of
their personal investments in keeping things as they are,
you may not be privy to their knowledge. That is probably
a good thing because all you really need to rely on right
now is your own inner guidance. That is definitely a
spiritual muscle that needs some of your attention right
now.*

*Energy is what everything is made up of. Even events that
take place while you walk this planet are only there
because you gave it your attention, and attention is
energy. If you don't like something, stop giving it energy
and it will die. It has to die because energy is what is
sustaining every event and everything in your life.
Remember what you give energy to will appear on your
viewing screen. Actually, energy is how everything is
measured within your mind and on this side of the veil.*

*On your planet there are numerous ways you measure
energy, calories, BTUs, PSIs, etc. But what you are really
measuring is thoughts because thoughts are the energy
that make up things and events on your planet. Your
planet is just a mirror of your collective consciousness.
When you harbor anger, the inability to forgive, greed,*

and thoughts of lack, your personal world will mirror back to you these very things in your life, which allows you to continue to feel this way. A wise person recognizes that all your external events are simply an outpouring of your internal dialogues taking place within your mind. This is why there is more turbulent weather than ever before, more destruction, more personal battles, more wars; all escalating now because of the mass internal struggle taking place within and Mother Earth must mirror those thoughts back to you.

If you would look at your relationships to others the same way you look at Mother Earth, then you can get a clearer picture of why She is reacting this way. Think of a time when you have done something terribly wrong to another. Hopefully, you learned a valuable lesson from the interaction, one that you won't likely repeat, and also through these experiences, you would have learned a different way to interact with that particular person. The more you interact in a loving way with others, the more your interactions will mirror back your newfound purpose. Mother Earth is no exception.

When you do something destructive to Mother Earth such as an oil spill, She feels, and reacts accordingly. Remember, if the world is a mirror of your thoughts, then when you go inside and change your thoughts, the world, and the oil spill included can now be looked at differently. Remember, it is told that when you name something, that is what it will be for you. If you name the oil spill bad, nothing good can come from it. Because of the spill there will be people in power who will force companies to look more closely at other sources to generate power on your planet. Once this is accomplished you will look back and thank BP for these changes that would have taken decades to unravel on your planet. Mother Earth can always heal Herself if we will allow Her. So too can you heal yourselves once you learn to allow Love to lead your way."

Your Responsibility in the Planetary Shifts:

"It is your responsibility, and I mean You the person reading this book right now, to share the information within this book with your brothers and sisters. You do not have the luxury of time. You can't wait for someone else to speak up. You are aware right now, so you can't walk the planet any longer and say you don't know. These shifts, and they are all energetic shifts, are all good, but as mentioned before, maybe too good for most. The energy of Love which is coming into the planet is being turned up to a level never experienced before. This energy will not dissipate, but will reach its peak between late 2014 and early 2015 and stay at that level.

This increase in the energy that is forthcoming, for those unaligned with who they are as children of God, will cause an enormous amount of fear and potential panic. The potential global impact of this energy coming into the planet could include some very chaotic behavior by those unwilling to accept the love being bestowed upon them.

Notice in the preceding paragraph how we used the words, 'potential,' and 'could,' and that was done intentionally. Could these influxes of energy cause power to be disrupted? Of course it can. Could it cause a solar energy fluctuation that would result in major communication brake-down? Of course it could. If you are guided to put provisions away for a period of disruption, then follow that guidance. If you are guided otherwise, follow that guidance as well. If you are coming from a place of love, you will be provided for under all circumstances.

But if you have put provisions away because of fear you will simply add to the fear already prevalent and encompassing the planet. Our ultimate desire, and we cannot stress this too often, is that you align yourself with who you are as a child of God. If enough truly miracle-

172

minded people make this shift, the ushering in of a new world will be nothing more than a speed bump.

Any potential disruptions would NOT be caused by the energy coming in but the fear generated as a result of the energy that is coming here. It is imperative that you motivate your brothers and sisters through LOVE and not fear. If you motivate and deliver any messages coming from fear, then the only thing that will have been accomplished is to unleash a wave of fear that could potentially cause long-term irreversible consequences. Please reread what was just written. Stay in the energy of love and ask God to speak through you to deliver these messages as He will know what is best to say to each person with whom you speak.

But ready or not, a new world is going to be ushered in. It is our goal and our deepest wish to have it ushered in, welcomed, and embraced, with love. For those that can welcome this shift – and notice how we used 'shift' as singular because there is only one shift to Joy for each of you this – will allow indescribable feelings of joy for each of you and your purpose for being here will be revealed to you.

People of your planet live by contrast. You job will be to lovingly explain that the energy coming in is love, and that it is all good. To many this love can cause a contrasting feeling because they are not used to being in a frequency of love. Show them that by connecting to who they are as a child of God that these shifts will feel wonderful, and the outcome will be a world filled with love. This new world will be a place void of, 'This is mine and that is yours, and I must protect what is mine.'

In your new world, wars will no longer exist, and people will be able to look into another's eyes and heal them. Acquiring things will be done for the community and not for individual needs. We laugh as we write 'individual needs' because after this shift you will see that you are one with all that is. Moving forward, individual needs will be something one would have to read about in history books and find that it took place before the new world was formed.

People will want to share. It will be enjoyable to live in a community that depends on everyone to do their part. The only emotion acceptable now will be love. Now one can see how many institutions will vanish – police, prisons, hospitals, just to name a few. I am here to tell you with great certainty, and this is frightening to most, that the last thing anyone needs is something else to be fearful of. Each message we are giving you is done in such a way so that you will to want to embrace being co-creators with God. Stop making choices coming from insanity and be part of the most joyous occurrence that has ever unfolded on any planet.

You will need to gently show others the benefits of connecting to who they are as a child of God. But you can't show them who they are as a child of God, if you aren't totally connected to who you are as a child of God. Your soul is crying out for you in an evolutionary fashion to change things, to expand, to move higher, and to understand. You are to bring these changes into manifestation from a place of equality and respect for each human being who has chosen to be on the planet at this time. They are no longer going to settle for "Do as I say, not as I do." Be that One!"

Paradigm Shifts:

"Paradigm shifts usually only occur on your planet when the old ways no longer work. But for most, as long as they believe there is one more way within the old order that might work, most will want to try it. It is only when those options have been exhausted that one is willing to try something completely different. It is like the energy that most on your planet use to transport yourselves about. As long as what you currently use is still available you really don't seek another alternative.

But the waiting for the last option to be exhausted sets one up for fear to surely follow. In one sense that is good because it puts you in a panic mode, and this makes you open to try something completely different. That is what a paradigm shift is – something completely different from the norm. Why not let the Voice for Truth guide you into what is best for you, your brothers and sisters, and Mother Earth. If you do that daily, one doesn't have to experience all the drama that could take place on your planet. Remember, pain is individual, but you can also experience pain as a collective consciousness. You can choose to be connected to the mass fear consciousness, or not. That is simply your choice. You can also choose to listen to the Voice for Truth which will provide an experience of love and joy. Be that one!

Power Shifts:

"There is energy coming into the planet that is available to everyone. It is like the sun that circles your planet. The energy of the sun is available to all and affects everyone regardless if they are aware or oblivious. The same is true of the energy that is the core source of each individual. It is the energy that sustains every function of

175

the body, and every plant, animal, fish, etc. This is also applicable to inanimate objects.

This energy that your scientists are aware of and can measure is increasing. The dial, so to speak, is constantly being turned up because of the imperative nature of the planetary shifts that will be taking place. One must align with this God energy or the disconnection could cause one to feel like one is dying. Actually, one aspect of you is dying, but only the old you with your old ways of interacting that will no longer be acceptable in your new world."

Chapter 18: The Responsibility of the Enlightened

The Responsibility of the Enlightened:

"The responsibility of the majority that knows what will be taking place is enormous. We must stress how important it is for those who know what is coming to remain connected to The Voice of Truth. You will need to stay focused on your alignment with who you are as a child of God. It will be your responsibility to help those still asleep and in denial with what is taking place. Each encounter will need to be highly individualized because of the varying frequency levels of those still asleep.

Your role will be to give them another way of looking at what is taking place in their life. Most will be ready because the pain will be so severe that they will seek out alternative ways. You will be that alternative. You will because you have heard and can now offer loving guidance in a manner that they can understand. Once again, you will be guided as to what to say, to whom, and how. But we need your eyes, feet, hands, mouth and ears to deliver these messages.

You can observe others in need by the mere fact that they are in fear, and this will signal to you that they are afraid of love. If they are in fear, then the last thing you want to do is to increase their fear. That is why We are asking you to allow us to guide you to help your brothers or sisters. In your next encounter with a different individual We might guide you in an entirely different mode because they are at a different energy level. Be kind to yourself, you cannot fail. Your role is to offer your guidance in a manner in which the recipient can understand. This will not be hard as long as you stay focused and remember you are a vortex for love and just the messenger."

Staying in the Love of Oneness:

"It is imperative that you stay focused on your role in ushering in a new world. Once you have experienced this Love and accepted your part in bringing in this new world the slightest disconnection could cause you excruciating pain. This doesn't mean you have done anything wrong, only that your vibrational level has dropped. Be glad you can feel the difference so when you feel the pain you can use this knowledge as a simple reminder to realign your thoughts back to the higher frequency of Love.

There are numerous ways to maintain your focus. The two most important times of the day are right before you go to sleep, by setting your intention to end the day by saying something as simple as, 'This day is over, it is done. If there were any egoic thoughts attached to any interactions between myself and my brothers and sisters, I ask for them to be removed.' When you awake in the morning ask for guidance in what your role for the – day should be and – when feasible throughout the day ask for guidance. To maintain your alignment when you speak, ask the Holy Spirit to speak for you. There are many other ways to stay in our Oneness; listening to certain music helps raise your frequency or you can meditate, stretch, take deep breaths, or do yoga. Daily mantras are also extremely helpful.

Remember to give each interaction a divine purpose. If you do those things you will go through these shifts with very little difficulty which will allow you to be available to assist your fellow brothers and sisters. One shouldn't make your tools for raising your frequency ritualistic, but a steady focus will eventually allow your subconscious mind to take over and match these frequencies as they becomes a part of who you are. Ask for guidance from whomever you call God; grant forgiveness to yourself and others to release your fears. And most of all, be kind and loving to yourself during any trials and tribulations you may experience."

Potential Challenges:

"There is virtually an endless array of challenges facing this current generation that has recently entered adulthood. As I stated previously, the World War II generation was called the greatest generation, but I tell you this new generation will surpass all others. They will usher in a new world, a world past generations couldn't have dreamed of. A world where equality becomes the norm, loving oneself, loving others, and giving to the planet more that they take. Now that is a paradigm shift!

Remember that your Mother Earth will mirror the majority reactions to the changes. Therefore, if there is a major resistance to this shift, that will cause the planet to bring about physical changes which will eventually help in ushering in the new world. Your responsibility is to become a part of the collective willingness to usher in this new world to reduce the severity of these shifts.

Ushering in a new world with its challenges could cause some of your fellow enlightened ones to feel like they are in the minority or outcasts. Please remember that all great teachers from your past who called for worldly changes were mocked or considered radical by non-visionaries of those times. Ushering in a new world is rather radical and many may react in the same way. Remain strong and focused on being that One!

Ways We Can Assist Others:

"When these shifts start taking place, there will be those that will come to you in dire need of help. Many will come reluctantly, but come they will. Your role is to remain centered in why you are here and then allow yourself to be the vortex for the Love of God that flows through you. You really don't need to seek out others. Don't look for people to fix. The people that need your help and are ready to receive the love you have to offer will be guided to you.

You might also be guided to give them shelter, help out physical, or financially because of some economic upheaval or planetary catastrophe. The ways you may be needed are endless, but when they come to you it will be no accident. Those that are destined to meet during these events will be brought together. Then you will see that your allowing yourself to be that vortex for Love now allows those that you helped to help others who still have forgotten who they are.

It is imperative that you listen and guide those that you help to help others. If you help one who doesn't pass it along, little is accomplished. We will guide you in this process, just remain open and realize that nothing is your responsibility except to be a channel for Love."

Ways We Can Help Our Communities:

"When these shifts start taking place, communities will play more significance in your lives than they have presently. There is no need for you to feel you have to isolate yourself from the world to keep yourself safe. You might feel another's pain/fear in no way has any bearing on you. Shame on yourself!!! You lack the trust that God has given you.

When you have accepted who you are as a glorious child of God, you will have such a strong innate desire to share that Love with your brothers and sisters. This Love cannot be contained and must go forth – it is in Love's nature. Because of this growing love coming into your planet, communal living will become the norm. At first communal living might occur because of economic or survival reasons, but that is fear-based thinking, and lacks the proper motivation that We are trying to bring forth.

When you come from love, communal living will mirror the love that you all are. True equality that this world has never experienced will become commonplace, and sharing with others will be part of your new being. Ask the mighty Voice for Truth to show you how looking into your brothers' and sisters' eyes, and seeing them, allows you to really see into their souls. It would be good practice to take some time and just look into someone's eyes for the singular purpose of seeing the God in YOU. When you can do that, you will have remembered who you are. Be that One!"

One cannot understand
Love, until one becomes
Love.

Chapter 19: The New World Order

Embracing the Changes:

"Changes to your planet are imperative. The old ways of interacting with our brothers and sisters have not brought anyone the peace your soul so desperately seeks. Remember these changes are needed. The world is old. It mirrors the collective consciousness of what permeates the planet. Because of the constant external and internal battles taking place, it wears down the world and all of the things in it. You no longer have the luxury of time to correct this disconnect to your Creator.

When you embrace these changes, your life will begin to flow rather easily – We might add. It will have to flow easily because you will be connected in ways you never have experienced before this change. As you say on your planet, 'In the flow.' Like a river – when you go with its natural flow you move along easily, but when you try to paddle against, it, you will wear yourself out. Well, the race consciousness has, for the vast majority, been going against the natural flow since the creation of the planet. This will and must CHANGE!

Once again, it is crucial that you embrace the planetary shifts, not only for your peace but the peace for all your brothers and sisters who remain asleep.

How the Changes will impact Our Lives:

"The energy coming into the planet will invoke changes to your planet and affect everyone on the planet when

these changes start to play out. You will no longer be able to deny them; you will feel them physically and emotionally. As mentioned in my first book, there will be changes that you can't even conceive of at the present time.

Your monetary system as you know it will change and living quarters for most will change, but the biggest change for will be the emotional changes. The giving up on 'I do this for you and you do this for me,' will vanish in the new world.

The future is still unwritten in the truest sense, and you will constantly rewrite your future daily. Embrace this new energy of Love coming into the planet. Accept your role of being the Vortex of Love, and the future will mirror that Love back to you. And with that Love, your Joy will be painted as a brush of Love on your planet that words cannot describe."

Changes in Your Communication with Others:

"'Your communication,' We are so happy to bring up this subject. Most people's communication skills are in the pre-kindergarten level. You still use your five senses to communicate, as your forefathers have done. This energy that is coming in will allow you to communicate in ways normally 'reserved' for physics. You will be able to look at someone and know what they are thinking. You will be able to scan their body and see what is out of alignment that is causing them discomfort. You will be able to diagnose the treatment that is best for the individual, given where they are at on the ladder back to God at the time.

You will be able to communicate with your higher power. When people have accepted their role, these new ways in communicating with each other will come from a place of Love. These powers will not be abused because at that level of awareness abuse and deception are not even an option. At this level there is only Love. All of these visions of your future are difficult to grasp right now because everything you have seen up this point has shown you different alternatives. Embrace it and enjoy it. The best days of your past will become the mundane days in your future."

Changes Within Our Communities:

"Changes within your communities will look entirely different from the way they have been for you so far. As mentioned previously there will be more communal living, and the way you communicate with each other will change significantly

Your monetary system will look different in the future, as there will be more bartering for goods and services. We struggle with the word 'barter' as it still has a 'giving-to-get' tag attached with it. Actually, the bartering will be done with love, and whatever one needs, the other will gladly supply because they know their true source is God. You will give gladly because you are now Love and you cannot withhold. It is your nature to give, and if you don't, you will die. Not necessarily in the sense of laying down your body, but die as in losing the essence of who you are. And that is the greatest death of all."

Changes in Our Technologies:

"The changes in your technologies will definitely bring green solutions. This is probably the greatest cause for concern for those in power on your planet. Remember I

stated that the world mirrors your thoughts. Since we think in a limited fashion, your Mother Earth mirrors those thoughts. But in the new world your thoughts will be in alignment with love, and that love is unlimited and produces abundance. Therefore, your technology will be completely renewable.

With this new way of generating energy to harness what will be needed on the planet, Mother Earth will heal herself. There will no longer be the need for your planet to cleanse itself from the garage being thrown on her, because love will now be the only emotional exchange between those on the planet. Until certain renewable sources for the planet become available, there will be those that can literally manifest what the community needs through the power of thought. Eventually that is the way all communities will be modeled. But until that occurs there will be a mixture of both."

Chapter 20: Evolving While Being in Oneness

Being Mindful:

"Unless you are mindful of whom you are as a glorious child of God you will feel disconnected during the ushering in of your new world. This requires the paradigm shift in consciousness that is presently occurring. Stop where you are right now and ask yourself, 'Am I really happy in how my life is unfolding?' Be honest!

You are being called to assist to bring about your new world order. In order to do that you, must be mindful and start making conscious choices that move you towards where we are going. Be alert to who you really are and stop reacting to the drama and stimuli that only the current world order can offer.

You were put here to be a co-creator with your Creator. 'Co-creator' means equality, not be subservient to a Voice. Make choices coming from Love; do them with Honor, Compassion, and Excitement. Start practicing this concept with mundane things, like brushing your teeth. Then try it on something you have a little more emotional investment in, and then when something "big" happens, you can use the same formula you employed earlier.

Each thought you have creates energy, and, as such, it goes out into the world and impacts the frequencies of those around you. Different thoughts cause your bodies to vibrate at different frequencies depending upon whether your thoughts are positive or negative. Positive thoughts produce higher frequency energy ranges and negative thoughts produce lower frequency. These energies are felt both within your bodies and then extend out beyond them as well. So your thoughts can impact others and their thoughts can impact you.

According to Dr. David Hawkins's map of consciousness, there are different frequencies of consciousness, ranging from zero at death to 1000 at Unity with God. See Chart below:

*Consciousness	Level	DNA Activation Level
Unity with God	1000	13% - 100%
Ascension	900	11% – 12 %
Illumination	800	10%
Enlightenment	700	9%
Equanimity	600	8%
Reverence	500	7%
Intelligence	400	6% - 7%
Optimism	300	5% - 6%
Trust	200	4% - 6%
Fear	100	0% - 4%
Death	0	0

*Qualitative and Quantitative Analysis and Calibration of the Levels of Human Consciousness, David R. Hawkins, M.D., PhD. Veritas Publishing

"While ushering in a new world, a paradigm shift will need to occur in each person within your communities. The paradigm shift is currently taking place now, and unless you start remembering who you are as a glorious child of God, you will continue to feel a disconnection. Stop where you are right now and ask yourself, 'Am I happy in how my life is unfolding?' Be honest! You must be mindful. You must start making conscious choices and stop reacting to the stimuli the world of the ego offers.

You were put here to be a co-creator with your Creator. Co-creator means equality. You were not meant to be subservient to a Voice. Make choices coming from Love. Do them with Honor, Compassion, and Excitement. Begin

by practicing with mundane things. Brush your teeth with Love, Honor, Compassion and Excitement, and then when something 'big' happens, you can apply the same formula you employed with the little things and it will then work, as it has become second nature.

To become mindful you are going to have to be vigilant in your thinking. Print or make up a daily mantra for yourself, something that will remind you to stay focused on why you are here and what you have to do today. Be kind and gentle with yourself. As you are in the human experience, therefore you will forget sometimes. Please remember there is nothing wrong with that. If you make a mistake, don't be hard on yourself, just try and do better the next time. Write down reminders for yourself. If need be, use whatever means works for you to remember your daily mantra. Say your mantra out loud and feel it. Don't just say it, but really feel it. It is in the feeling of what your mantra says that will then bring it into manifestation."

Teaching Our Brothers and Sisters:

"The word 'teaching' implies that someone doesn't know something, and that another person does know what's lacking and can then provide that information to the original person. You will not teach your brothers and sisters in a sense the world looks at teaching. Your role will be to remind them what they already know. Remember, in the new world order there is only equality; all knowledge will be available to all. There are those that know and those who have forgotten. But what has been forgotten can be remembered, given a little willingness.

You have a saying on your planet, 'When the student is ready, the teacher will appear.' And that is so true. When one of your brothers or sisters is ready to remember what they have forgotten, you can show them because you have remembered. For those who have remembered, you cannot not help but awaken your sleeping brothers and sisters. So go forth and teach them what they have forgotten. You can do that with word, thought, or by just being who you are as God created you. That is always the best teacher, leading by example. Be that One!"

Increasing Our Vibrations of Love:

"The only way to increase and maintain the vibration of Love is by being connected to Love. You can't be listening, doing, or acting out of alignment with Love and expect to hear the mighty Voice for Truth. Given where most of you are, you learn through contrast. So when you feel or experience something that doesn't generate an emotion of pure love, simply realize you have temporarily forgotten who you are. But you can remember, given the willingness to do so. It is time to stop talking about love and analyzing love, and start being that love.

When another's joy brings you joy, you have arrived. When you give something to someone and see the joy it brings them and share in that same joy, you have arrived. There are numerous modalities that will help in your awareness of who you are, but none will work unless the goal of ushering in this new world is your main focus. If you were to ask us which modality is right for you We would tell you that you will know which one is right for you when it no longer matters what anyone else chooses. When you choose love without regard to what anyone else does, then you are on the right path in your journey."

The New Way of Being:

"To usher in a new world the old antiquated ways of interacting with ourselves, our brothers, sisters, and Mother Earth have to change drastically. Hopefully, we have seen how the male-dominated way of wining at all cost of taking more than you give, greed, the monetary system, the medical system, and reciprocal relationships have been found lacking for most people. All one has to do is just take a look outside. Surely no one can say this is how it should be. Most people sleepwalk through life not knowing that they even have an option. They make decisions by default, deciding not to decide, and they have become reactors to the world instead of accepting what they have come to do, as co-creators in the ushering in of a new world.

Be honest, pain and contrast dominates your world. Have you ever truly been content in all areas of your life? You work to bring you the illusionary security you think money brings. You watch others play sports and exercise as if they are gods. Foolishness to such thoughts! You are sustained by the Love of God. It is only when you have accepted your purpose for being here that will you have any glimmer of true security."

Honoring Mother Earth:

"Mother Earth has been neglected, ignored, and used. But that is no different than the way we have treated ourselves and our brothers and sisters. In ushering in a new world, you will stop taking more than you are receiving and start giving more than you are taking. It will feel like the most natural thing to do because Love must give. When you receive love, it is always in an amount that you must share because your heart will be overflowing.

Because you have started honoring yourself, that energy will flow over into honoring Mother Earth. She will speak to you in the wind, and you will feel her messages with your feet, and you will see what she is trying to tell you through the magnificent paintings of the seasons on a canvas of love. Giving will no longer be associated with the perceived lack that usually accompanies the act of giving. One now looks out and can only see oneself, and since that oneself is connected to God, one can only see God. When one looks at Mother Earth, one sees oneself and asks the question, 'What does Mother Earth need in this moment, and how can I give it with Honor, Compassion, and Excitement?'"

Chapter 21: Life as it was Intended

Suggestions for Family:

"Family will become extremely important, but first we must define family in a new way. The word 'family' will take on new meaning in the new world of love which includes everyone you come into contact with. The closest you can come to that type of love right now, given where most of you vibrate, is the parent/child relationship. And we mean a healthy parent/child relationship – we realize some have not experienced being raised by loving parents.

Your future family and communal living quarters by today's standards would be viewed as 'cramped.' But the need to have my house, my car, my, my, will dissipate because your identification as who you are will no longer be tied to things that make up your persona. Sharing will be natural, and the joy of one is the joy of all. So you won't mind living in smaller spaces because you will be enjoying the interactions of your fellow occupants in a way you never have before. For most, these are just words, but in the awakening they will be lived and felt at a level we truly cannot explain.

WE ARE TRYING TO SHARE WITH YOU WHAT SOME OF YOU AREN'T PRESENTLY READY FOR. BUT IF YOUR MIND IS AWARE THAT THESE THINGS WILL BE HAPPENING, IT CAN FACILITATE THE AWAKENING OF YOUR HEART. BE THAT ONE!"

Suggestions for Community:

"Communities will no longer compete with other communities for jobs or natural resources. They will be coming from a place of 'How can I help my brothers and sisters who live in my community?' as well as those that live in other communities. You might be guided to share what you have and what you have learned. Teach them by painting a picture of how others can live their daily lives with Honor, Compassion, and Excitement.

As always, ask the Holy Spirit what is the most loving and kind thing you can do for your community and others that might temporarily need assistance. Notice we used the word 'temporarily' because sometimes helping others before was usually a way to get others to need you so you could control them. This is a new paradigm and the helping of others can only come from love. They will only need your assistance temporarily because once they embrace their Oneness, they will be living in abundance as God intended."

The Impact of Living a Life in Oneness:

"The impact of living a life in Oneness cannot be described with words. Picture the happiest moment of your life and take it to an infinite number, and then you might get a glimmer as to what living in Oneness means. When this occurs, and it really is only a thought away, the raising of the next generation would be like watching a fairy tale that a child might read.

Right now we show our children books that depict racism, segregation, depression, etc. because that was the way we have historically interacted with our brothers and sisters. In the new world you won't show them anything about how we used to live because their vibration could not even conceived of such things – given where children raised in Oneness will vibrate. They will own nothing because they own everything. They will give because they have everything, and they will love all because they love themselves. Be kind to yourself with these angels of God, they will be your greatest teachers. They will mirror God in the flesh."

The Next Generation Raised in Oneness:

"This new generation that you are presently birthing into manifestation will have a place prepared for them that would resemble the Garden of Eden. They will see Oneness because they are Oneness. They will communicate in ways you have never conceived of at the present time. As spoken of many generations before, this generation will mirror Heaven on Earth.

You need to put aside what that will look like because most minds are not ready! Even if we drew an outline, it would make little difference. The reason for the last sentence is the outline would only include words that have feelings associated with them, like love, joy, happiness, peace, family, and sharing. You mind needs things it can see because if it has something it can see, then it magically believes that it can see the results.

Don't concern yourself about future generations because your function is here and now. Ask what your role should be in ushering in a new world. Realize that your part actually holds greater importance than the next generation. They will have everything before them, they will be ready. Your function is the ushering in of a new world. We will be with you step by step. Remember, you agreed before incarnating at this time that you would lay the foundation for a new world. We hold you in our arms, and our faith in you has never wavered. I know We have constantly said, "Be that One!" Because we know you are that One!"

Chapter 22: Collapsing Time to Completeness

Collapsing Time to Completeness:

"Within the frequency of time there are individual needs, wants and a life that is lived by comparison. Fear is rooted in time because of the inherent lack associated within the frequency of time. As soon as one starts the awakening process and begins to associate time with emotions that don't bring the joy you are desperately seeking, the collapsing of time begins to take on major importance. With this is your hearts, you can seek better options to bring forth the desired results.

The collapsing of time will be done in stages at the beginning. Every time you remember who you are, in every instant that you offer love, you have removed the dependence one places on the need to listen to the egoic mind. With each act of forgiveness, time is drawn closer to eternity. The more one is attached to the egoic mind, the longer between thought and the manifestation of the thought. When one puts more importance on the Voice of Truth, then that thought and the manifestation of that thought are felt accordingly.

When you choose to live with love more than living from fear, you can then begin to give everyone and everything a divine purpose. With your newfound joy you will start to share this love because sharing is a natural aspect of love. With each decision to see through the eyes of love, the collapsing of time occurs and will expedite itself until the need to live in a frequency of time dissipates."

Collapsing Time More Quickly:

*"To expedite the removal of living in a fear-based system
of time, there are numerous modalities at your disposal.
There is none of greater importance than another, but we
would offer some suggestions. Listening to classical or
meditation music that registers at a high frequency or
doing meditation, yoga, forgiveness, stretching,
breathing, and countless other practices will work.*

*Begin by being aware of any spiritual thought systems
you currently practice that don't depict God as pure love.
Also be aware of any thought systems that requires a
sacrificing of something to get something. If you truly
desire to be part of the awakening process, truly desire
the peace of God more than correcting or judging others,
then you will be open to the modality that is right for you
at the present time.*

*The fastest way is always through the dynamics of
forgiveness. And when time is over, forgiveness will just
be a memory, because once you are past forgiveness,
there is only Love. You are now part of this ushering in of
a new world of Love, and you will only have one desire –
that of showing others how they too can feel what you
feel. Be that One!"*

Chapter 23: Be That One

Be That One:

"When we ask you to 'Be that One!' we are asking you to really listen to the message that is being presented to you. Then we will ask you to be that One that carries Our message into the world. Your job is simply to say that you are ready. You don't have to know how or by what means, but simply say something in the order of, 'Okay, if the Holy Spirit asks me to do this thing, I will head in that direction.'

Actually, all that will be required is for you to be that One is the willingness to be that One. This is a powerful and simple statement. Be the One that will be a vortex to allow the Voice for Truth to flow through you in ways that will bring yourself and your brothers and sisters great joy. In the doing of this most divine service, you have already accomplished what you are supposed to be doing at this time in the unfoldment on your planet. You also allow others to be that One."

Embrace All That You Are:

"Indeed, embrace all that you are, honor all that you are, and extend all that you are. It is time to step out of your small self that your ego thinks gives you some resemblance of peace. It is time to reach the level of commitment where you see your role as extraordinary. It is time to stop playing with your little 'Me' that is only capable of trying to survive. It is time to accept Our invitation and take your rightful place by making a full commitment for this extraordinary expression that is

presently unfolding on your planet. It is time to allow the mind and heart to participate in the quickening process of collapsing time. With your assurance given to your Creator the shortening of the illusions of time becomes immeasurable. Be that One!

Most of your brothers and sisters have come under the spell of the illusionary concepts that permeate your planet. This makes the world a fearful place, a planet where survival encompasses every minute of the day. For those who have allowed the egoic mind to rule, have played small, and sought reciprocal relationships, they will see no other paths before them. Be that One that shows them how pitiful their perception of the world they see is. Be that One that shows them another path back to the place they never left! Be that One that walks hand and hand on the most glorious journey ever taken on your planet!"

Awakening Others:

"In this period of transformation your role is to awaken those who have forgotten who they are. Your brothers and sisters remain asleep while they have forgotten. They need a gentle touch from someone to awake them. Be that One that allows them to see the face of God in your eyes!

For when you accept your part, your heart will be thrown open, and the joy you will experience is so immense, your words can be no longer contained. You can only experience this feeling. Yet it takes vigilance and much discipline to always remember during each day, hour, and interaction to never fall asleep or forget your purpose. The temptations of the world will always be there, for that is the purpose you have given it. Be that One who gives the world another purpose!

Many of you will quicken your ability to communicate with those I refer to as 'We.' While you still have a body, honor and love one another. Remember their cries for help mirror yours. You can no longer ignore what your eyes show you. Being ordinary and blending in will no longer be an option. The pain will be too intense. You will have to come forth and seize this opportunity in the unfoldment of your planet. You will be able to play out the greatest drama ever experienced on any dimension. You have agreed to be part of laser-beam purification. Hold on, buckle up, enjoy the ride, the train has left the station. BE THAT ONE!

Fail not your fellow brothers and sisters. Look lovingly upon them and accept your part in the unfoldment of a new world. What you are becoming, and this is a core DNA change you will go through, will allow you to joyfully proclaim to the entire world this transmutation that must take place. Let them see the peace in your eyes. Show them what must take place to usher in this new world. Because in order for some to believe the new world order has taken place, they must witness others living in Oneness. BE THAT ONE!"

Living in Sonship:

"Your life now must become a life of service to the Sonship regardless of the individual form in which it is expressed. You are here to tip the balance in your mind to one of totally experiencing who you are as this glorious child of God. In this process of awakening you will tip the scales in other minds because you are always one with those you have gazed upon with your loving eyes. That is your purpose. BE THAT ONE!

Once you start this journey, a transfiguration will take place in your soul. This transfiguration will overlap every

201

*area of your life, and the old antiquated ways will become
a distant memory like a toy you played with as a child.
You are the forerunners of a generation where words will
no longer be needed, where thoughts will instantly
produce the desired results. This generation will hear the
call as all others have, but this generation will be
different – it will answer the call. You will see and feel the
deep connection to your brothers and sisters and will
leave no one to their own demise. BE THAT ONE!*

*As mentioned, the world has to be spoon-fed in the
awakening process. Also it was mentioned that the future
is always subject to change because you are creating your
tomorrows today. The race and gender consciousness of
the planet as mention earlier will determine your future.
Because of that, additional information will be given after
these shifts have taken hold and We see how well your
brothers and sisters have welcomed the love that is
streaming into the planet.*

*Therefore, the next book that will be brought forth from
the other side will be unveiled sometime in 2014. Of
course, even that is subject to change because if the vast
majority welcomes this shift with love then the messages
can be brought forth sooner. If fear is the dominate
emotion, then We will probably wait until 'the dust
settles.'*

2012 and Beyond:

*"2012 is not an ending but a springboard into the
birthing of a new world. The reason for the writing of this
book in a gentle, soothing fashion is to bring one's mind
into a place of knowing only Love is real. Love must be
delivered to you in stages so that the power of this Love
doesn't increase the fear already deeply buried in your
mind. It has to be done in a gentle fashion or fear will*

increase, and thus minimize the purpose of the messages this books must bring forth.

By the mere fact that you are reading this book, at some level you have given your consent to your Creator to allow this transfiguration of your mind and soul to take this journey. So, as you read over each book and each chapter, all messages will be delivered in a gentle fashion, because a soft voice will allow the mind to ease into that place that knows only of Love.

Hopefully, what We are offering you is a way to soften your heart and mind and be more willing to be less fearful. Nothing We have said is meant to solicit fear. You are literally witnessing the forerunning effects of what is to come. Be that One that helps Us to usher in a new world!"

We give you these messages so you can individually prepare for these planetary shifts but, just as importantly, as each one of you raise your level of awareness you also raise it for the planet. Thus, it is our sincere wish that the planet will embrace these shifts as they would with a speed bump effect instead of hitting a brick wall.

For I have loved each of you with a Love that has no end. Anderson!"

Make sure you read Anderson's First Book:

Messages from Across the Unknown Sea

How to Navigate the Loss of a Life Taken Too Soon

ANDERSON SPEAKS

WRITTEN BY
Anderson Skaggs

AS COMMUNICATED TO
Gene Skaggs, Jr.

About the Author:

Gene grew up in the beautiful city of Key West, Florida. He moved to Nashville in 1979 with his wife and their oldest son Jason. That same week Gene attended a Unity church, with a guest speaker, whose topic for the day was A Course in Miracles.

Since that day Gene has been studying A Course in Miracles, and attending the Unity church. He is a certified PSYCH-K facilitator, has a private counseling practice, and has spoken at numerous Unity churches throughout the country. In addition he and Lucy have spoken at various Compassionate Friends Organizations, an organization for those who have lost a child. Gene has also led numerous grief recovery workshops. Gene also has written four books on A COURSE IN MIRACLES and this is his second book pertaining to messages Anderson has given him.

Gene feels everything he has done in his life has led up to this moment in time, where he has come together with Lucy, to deliver the messages that Anderson is revealing to him from the other side. It is his sincere wish that you take these messages that have come from Anderson, allow them to inspire you to live your life with Honor, Compassion, and Excitement.

For additional information about the author:
Websites: www.onemiracle.org and www.geneskaggs.com
Facebook: Gene Skaggs
Twitter: Anderson_Speaks

www.ingramcontent.com/pod-product-compliance
Lightning Source LLC
Chambersburg PA
CBHW051822090426
42736CB00011B/1612